THE SECRET OF CULTURE CHANGE

The SECRET OF CULTURE CHANGE

HOW TO BUILD AUTHENTIC STORIES THAT TRANSFORM YOUR ORGANIZATION

JAY B. BARNEY
MANOEL AMORIM
CARLOS JÚLIO

Berrett–Koehler Publishers, Inc.

Berrett-Koehler Publishers, Inc.
1333 Broadway, Suite 1000
Oakland, CA 94612-1921
Tel: (510) 817-2277
Fax: (510) 817-2278
www.bkconnection.com

ORDERING INFORMATION

Quantity sales. Special discounts are available on quantity purchases by corporations, associations, and others. For details, contact the "Special Sales Department" at the Berrett-Koehler address above.
Individual sales. Berrett-Koehler publications are available through most bookstores. They can also be ordered directly from Berrett-Koehler: Tel: (800) 929-2929; Fax: (802) 864-7626; www.bkconnection.com.
Orders for college textbook / course adoption use. Please contact Berrett-Koehler: Tel: (800) 929-2929; Fax: (802) 864-7626.

Distributed to the U.S. trade and internationally by Penguin Random House Publisher Services.

Berrett-Koehler and the BK logo are registered trademarks of Berrett-Koehler Publishers, Inc.

Printed in Canada

Berrett-Koehler books are printed on long-lasting acid-free paper. When it is available, we choose paper that has been manufactured by environmentally responsible processes. These may include using trees grown in sustainable forests, incorporating recycled paper, minimizing chlorine in bleaching, or recycling the energy produced at the paper mill.

Library of Congress Cataloging-in-Publication Data

Names: Barney, Jay B., author. | Amorim, Manoel, author. | Júlio, Carlos, author.
Title: The secret of culture change : how to build authentic stories that transform
    your organization / Jay B. Barney, Manoel Amorim, Carlos Júlio.
Description: First Edition. | Oakland, CA : Berrett-Koehler Publishers, [2023] |
    Includes bibliographical references and index.
Identifiers: LCCN 2022060637 (print) | LCCN 2022060638 (ebook) |
    ISBN 9781523004928 (paperback) | ISBN 9781523004935 (pdf) |
    ISBN 9781523004942 (epub) | ISBN 9781523004966 (audio)
Subjects: LCSH: Organizational change. | Leadership. | Management—
    Employee participation.
Classification: LCC HD58.8 .B379 20239 (print) |
    LCC HD58.8 (ebook) | DDC 658.4/06—dc23/eng/20221219
LC record available at https://lccn.loc.gov/2022060637
LC ebook record available at https://lccn.loc.gov/2022060638

First Edition

29 28 27 26 25 24 23   10 9 8 7 6 5 4 3 2 1

Book producer: Westchester Publishing Services
Cover designer: Adam Johnson

Contents

Preface

Everyone we know who has tried to change their organization's strategies sooner or later runs into the same problem: To realize the full potential of these new strategies, they usually must also change their organization's culture. This is true no matter where you work—in an established for-profit firm, in an entrepreneurial firm, in a not-for-profit organization, or even in a government agency. Typically, your current culture enables the implementation of your old strategies. It follows that if you are changing these old strategies, it is very likely that you will need to also change your old culture.

But what if you don't change your old culture when you are implementing your new strategies? As Peter Drucker was alleged to have said, when your old culture and new strategies are not aligned, then "Culture eats strategy for breakfast!"

So, great. You get it. To fully implement new strategies, you often need to change your organization's culture. But how do you change your old culture?

While much has been written about culture change, we have found much of it to be distant from the actual practice of culture change. By this, we aren't suggesting that prior work on culture change is without merit. Indeed, in this book we draw on many principles of culture change articulated in this prior work.

But we were looking for a more hands-on, practical approach that managers in any kind of organization, and at any level in an organization, could use to change their culture. And so we decided to ask managers how they went about changing their culture.

And what they told us was surprising.

Most successful culture-change efforts began when a business leader "built a story." Leaders built these stories by engaging in activities that clearly broke with a firm's cultural past, while providing a path to its cultural future. Moreover, these activities were authentic, "starred" the business leader in question, appealed to employees' hearts and heads, were often very theatrical, and led others in the organization to build their own stories.

This book shares 38 of these stories, culled from over 150 we collected from interviews with a large sample of business leaders. It also tells you how you can build your own stories to begin your own culture-change process, as well as why and when this approach to culture change will work.

We have seen these ideas applied in all kinds of firms—from global Fortune 500 companies to very small entrepreneurial firms, fast-growing technology companies, not-for-profit organizations, institutes of higher education, government agencies, and so forth. We have also seen these ideas applied at all levels in an organization—by CEOs, by functional vice presidents, by division general managers, by plant or office managers, by first-line supervisors, and by hourly workers with each other.

However, this book does not give you a list of stories you can tell to motivate culture change in your company. This is a book on story building, not storytelling, so you must build your own stories to change your own culture. We describe what attributes these stories need to have to be successful, but we cannot tell you what the content of these stories will be. That is up to you to create—although the numerous examples presented in this book will probably give you some ideas about the kinds of stories you might be able to build.

As you start building stories to change your organizational cultures, we'd love to hear from you about your experiences. What worked? What didn't work? What would you not change about this process? What would you change? You can share the stories you build to change your organizational culture on our website, CultureChangeSecret.com. We hope that this website will be a source for furthering our collective knowledge about story building and culture change.

So, good reading, and good luck in your own efforts to create the kind of culture that will enable you, and all with whom you work, to realize your and their full potential.

| Jay B. Barney | Manoel Amorim | Carlos Júlio |
| Park City, Utah, USA | Orlando, Florida, USA | São Paulo, Brazil |

Dedication

This book is dedicated to the many business leaders we interviewed who shared with us their culture-changing experiences. The names and backgrounds of those with stories in the book are presented here.

Fernando Aguirre—Owner and CEO, Erie Seawolves Baseball; Chairman, President, and CEO, Chiquita Brands; several General Manager, Vice President and President positions at Procter & Gamble; director on several boards.

Manoel Amorim—President and CEO, Abril Education; CEO, Globex; Managing Director, Consumer Business, Telefonica International; CEO, Telesp (Telefonica); General Manager, Procter & Gamble; director on several boards; National Advisory Council, Marriott School of Business.

Jeremy Andrus—CEO, Traeger Pellet Grills; Entrepreneur in Residence, Solamere Capital; President and CEO, Skull Candy.

Marise Barroso—Group Vice President, Avon; CEO, Marisa; CEO, Amanco Brazil; several board assignments.

Dan Burton—CEO, Health Catalyst; Managing Partner, HB Ventures; Head of Corporate Strategy, Micron Technology; director on several corporate boards; member of the National Advisory Council, Marriott School of Business.

Alberto Carvalho—Operating Partner, Advent International; Partner, CEO Coaching International; President, Procter & Gamble Brazil, Argentina, and Chile; Vice President, Global Gillette Business; CEO, The Art of Shaving; several board assignments; Advisor to the Center of Emerging Markets, Northeastern University.

Cliff Clive—Founder and CEO, MediNatura Inc.; CEO, Heel Inc.; CEO, Breville North America; General Manager, Power Bar, Nestlé; President, Consumer Health Americas, Roche Pharmaceuticals.

Ivan Sartori Filho—Partner, Mind Makers International; Vice President, SOMOS Education; Regional Director, Telefonica International; General Manager—Plastics and Coatings, Alcoa Brazil; York Business Unit Manager, Tenneco; Adjunct Professor, Catholic University in Rio de Janeiro.

Annette Friskopp—General Manager of PageWide Industrial Printing and Specialty Printing and Technology Global Business Units, HP Inc.; CEO and President, Zaptrio Inc.; Executive Vice President of a fleet management company (name kept confidential); board member, Out & Equal.

Melanie Healey—Group President, North America; Group President, Global Health and Feminine Care; President, Global Feminine Care and Adult Care; Vice President and General Manager, NA Feminine Care, Procter & Gamble; several corporate board assignments.

Brett Keller—CEO, COO, CMO, and VP of Marketing, Priceline; member of the National Advisory Council, Marriott School of Business.

Shane Kim—Interim CEO and Director, GameStop; several roles as Corporate Vice President and General Manager at Microsoft; several board assignments.

Brigitte Madrian—Dean and Marriott Distinguished Professor, Brigham Young University Marriott School of Business; Codirector, National Bureau of Economic Research, Household Finance Working Group; several board assignments.

Jamie O'Banion—Founder and CEO, Beauty Biosciences LLC; member of the National Advisory Council, Marriott School of Business.

Pete Pizarro—Managing Partner, SALT Venture Partners; President and CEO, Ilumno; Chairman and CEO, eLandia Group; CEO, Telefonica USA; several board assignments.

Stefano Retore—Founder, LemanVentures; President, Origination; member of Executive Council and Group Chief Risk Officer, Archer Daniel Midland Company; President, International and President Brazil, CHS Inc.; several corporate board assignments.

Dennis Robinson—President and COO, Mill Town Capital/Bousquet Enterprises; Managing Director, Envorso; Chief of Staff and Assistant Secretary of State, New Jersey; COO, Formula 1 Grand Prix of America; CEO at a major sports and entertainment venue (kept confidential); Assistant to the Athletic Director, University of Houston.

Scott Robinson—Managing Director, Robinson Resource Group; Founder, SearchWorks; Managing Partner, Kensington International; VP of Human Resources, Bally Gaming; Human Resources Director, Federal Signal Corporation.

Jeff Rodek—Chairman and CEO, Hyperion Solutions; President, Ingram Micro; SVP, Americas, FedEx; several board assignments; Senior Lecturer, Fisher College of Business.

Michael Schutzler—CEO, Washington Technology Industry Association; Executive Coach, CEOsherpa.com; CEO, Livemocha; CEO, Classmates.com; CEO, FreeShop; several corporate board assignments; Advisory Board member and part-time faculty, University of Washington Michael G. Foster School of Business.

Michael Speigl—Dealer Principal, Toyota and Subaru of Ann Arbor; Founder, Prep & Me; President, Williams Automotive Group; Managing Partner, Tampa Honda; Adjunct Professor, Stephen M. Ross School of Business, University of Michigan.

Mike Staffieri—COO, Senior Vice President, Kidney Care, and Vice President of Operations and New Center Development, DaVita, Inc.

Andy Theurer—CEO, President, and CFO, ARUP Laboratories.

Carl Thong—Serial Entrepreneur-Founder/President/Partner/ Managing Director of Sunstone Group, Momenta Group, BankingON, Re:start Banking, Dytan Health, and Dinning Buttler, among others; several board assignments; Adjunct Professor, Singapore Management University.

Greg Tunney—CEO, President, and Director, Manitobah Mukluks; Global President, Wolverine WorldWide; CEO, RG Barry Corporation; CEO, Phoenix Footwear Group; Adjunct Lecturer, Ohio State University; Adjunct Lecturer, David Eccles School of Business, University of Utah; several board assignments.

Steve Young—Chairman and Cofounder, Huntsman Gay Global Capital; former football player for the San Francisco 49ers and league Most Valuable Player, elected to the NFL Hall of Fame; sports commentator for Monday Night Football on ESPN; book author.

Stories in the Book

THE SECRET OF CULTURE CHANGE

CHAPTER ONE

Building Stories to Change Your Organization's Culture

H ere is what we know about the relationship among a firm's culture, its strategies, and its performance:

Organizations where culture and strategy align outperform organizations where culture and strategy do not align.

Of course, this doesn't mean that your organization's strategy is unimportant. Indeed, the history of business over at least the last 50 years or so is a history of the emergence and then the dominance of new and disruptive technological and business strategies in sector after sector.[1]

This pattern has emerged in numerous commercial industries, including retail sales (Sears, Walmart, Amazon), home entertainment (broadcast television, prerecorded videos and DVDs, streaming services), computers (mainframes, personal computers, smartphones), and so forth. This same pattern has also occurred in some not-for-profit and government sectors—for example, governments directly distributing foreign aid to the governments of less developed economies, international nongovernmental organizations (NGOs) providing these governments with loans, and NGOs directly funding entrepreneurial activities in these economies through microfinance.[2]

And yet, research over this same period of time has made it clear that to realize the full potential of these innovative strategies, they must be aligned with your organization's culture.[3] Your firm may have an exciting new product or technology, or an exciting new way to distribute or market this product or technology, but unless your organizational culture aligns with your strategies, its full potential will not be realized.

Thus, for example, if your business strategy focuses on selling highly innovative products or services to your customers, then you must have a culture that supports teamwork, creativity, and risk-taking among your employees. If it focuses on selling high-quality products or services, then you must have a culture that supports quality processes in all that you do. If it focuses on providing excellent customer service, then this kind of service must be central to your organization's culture.[4] And if your strategy focuses on helping entrepreneurs in developing economies, then your culture must celebrate profits as an outcome of economic development.[5]

Strategic and Cultural Misalignment

So, we all agree: to get the highest level of performance, your strategies and culture need to be aligned. But what if they aren't? What are your options?

First, you can change your strategies. While it may be possible to modify your strategies to some degree to more completely align with your culture, fundamentally changing your strategies so that they align with your culture can be a problem. For example, if your analysis of the market suggests that in order to optimize your performance you need to pursue, say, an innovative product differentiation strategy, and the culture you have in your organization does not support such a strategy, then abandoning this strategy may put the performance of your organization at risk. After all, you choose strategies because you are convinced that they will create competitive advantages for your firm.[6] Abandoning such strategies because they don't align with your culture can be very problematic.

Second, you can try to ignore this misalignment, perhaps hoping that—over time—your organization's culture will evolve in a way that will ultimately align with your strategy. However, our experience tells us that you usually do not have the luxury of time—you need to implement your strategies sooner, not later. And in the meantime, while you are waiting for your culture to evolve, your strategies direct your employees to do one thing while your culture tells them to do something else. In this setting—as Peter Drucker is alleged to have once observed—when there is a conflict between a firm's culture and its strategy, "Culture eats strategy for breakfast."

So, in the end, when there is a misalignment between your strategies and your culture, you often really only have one choice:

You need to change your culture!

The Culture-Change Problem

But how do you change your organization's culture? Great question!

Indeed, some of the world's leading thinkers on organizational change are skeptical about your ability to change your organization's culture. Consider, for example, John Kotter's views on culture change:

> One of the theories about change that has circulated widely over the past fifteen years might be summarized as follows: The biggest impediment to creating change in a group is culture. Therefore, the first step in a major transformation is to alter the norms and values. After the culture has been shifted, the rest of the change effort becomes more feasible and easier to put into effect. I once believed in this model. But everything I've seen over the past decade tells me it's wrong. Culture is not something that you manipulate easily. Attempts to grab it and twist it into a new shape never work because you can't grab it.[7]

Despite this pessimism, there are, of course, many books and articles that describe how to change an organization's culture.[8] Most of these apply one or another of currently popular models of organizational change to the problem of culture change.[9] And, as we will see, many of these change management models do have important implications for understanding and implementing culture change.

The Secret of Culture Change

However, our approach to understanding the problem of culture change did not start by examining the implications of these different change management models. Instead, we simply asked a large sample of business leaders what they did to change their organizational cultures. And it turns out that what these leaders told us is not emphasized in most prior work on culture change.

If you want to change your organization's culture, start by building stories.

This is the "secret" to changing your organization's culture—building stories.

In retrospect, the idea that building stories can be important in changing an organization's culture should not have been that surprising. After
all, an organization's culture is typically developed and diffused throughout an organization by the stories employees share about the firm and its
values and norms.[10] It follows that if you want to change your culture, you
need to change the stories that employees in your firm share with each other.

But how do you build culture-changing stories?

What the business leaders we interviewed told us is that you build
culture-changing stories by engaging in actions that are radically different
from your organization's current culture—activities that establish a clear
break with the past and that demonstrate a clear path to a new cultural
future. These actions then turn into stories that exemplify the culture you
are trying to create. These stories spread widely and rapidly throughout your
organization, as employees talk—first in whispers, and later with excitement
and enthusiasm—"Did you hear what our leader did?"

In short, the business leaders we spoke to didn't just "talk" about culture change. Nor did they just "walk" the culture change they hoped to create. Rather, these business leaders "walked" this culture change in a way
that "talked" to their entire organization. They did this by purposefully and
consciously and deliberately engaging in actions that built stories that exemplified the culture they wanted to create and stories that would rapidly
spread throughout their organization. For these business leaders, building
stories was "walking that talks."

We call this process "story building," and our research suggests that
building stories is usually the first step in changing your organization's culture. And changing your organization's culture is often critical in efficiently
and effectively implementing your strategies to realize their full potential.

Story Building, Not Storytelling

However, please do not confuse story building with storytelling. Of course,
storytelling is an important phenomenon in most organizations. Telling
simple, engaging, and inspiring stories is a great way to motivate and communicate with your employees.[11] A moving story about an athlete overcom-
ing seemingly insurmountable odds, or a political figure's struggle to right
some horrible wrong, or how an entrepreneur transformed an obscure business idea into a Fortune 500 enterprise are all great.

We can even learn about how to build culture-changing stories from people who have done this in their own organizations. Indeed, this is the fundamental premise of this book.

But this book is *not* about using these stories to try to change your organization's culture. We do not expect that any of the stories told in this book will change your organization's culture. You can retell them, if you would like, to exemplify the story-building process. But to change your culture, you must build your own stories. We can tell you—based on our research—the attributes that the stories you build must have if they are going to change your culture. But, in the end, they must be stories that you build. In short:

Culture change is about you *being the culture you want to create by acting in ways consistent with the new culture and inconsistent with the current culture.*

You build these stories, even if you don't fully know what that future culture will be, and even if almost everyone else in the organization thinks you might be mad. Culture change is about building stories that exemplify the culture you are trying to create. Consider the following example.

A Story-Building Example

STORY 1.1 "Using a Customer Service Failure to Change an Organization's Culture" ·
Manoel Amorim as CEO at Telesp (Telefonica)

Prior to my becoming the CEO of the Brazilian telecom company Telesp, the company was highly regulated by the government. Our only goals were to meet government-mandated service standards and to do so as efficiently as possible. And we were good at reaching these goals. We had met the service standards set by the government before any of the other Brazilian telecoms and had never been more profitable.

During this time, the company had developed a very strong top-down, command-and-control culture. The government told top managers what they needed to do, top management told employees what they needed to do, and employees did whatever they were told. While very efficient in enabling Telesp to reach its government-mandated goals, this culture had led to a very isolated, even elitist, top management team. As one example of this elitist culture: no regular employees were allowed to be in the same elevator as the CEO.

At some point, it became clear that the competitive situation at Telesp was about to change. Our government-protected monopoly in the São Paulo market was going to end, and we were going to have to compete for our customers' business. It was obvious to me that we were going to need to shift from a command-and-control culture focused on reaching government service requirements to a customer service–oriented culture focused on getting and keeping customers with new telecom products and high levels of customer support.

One of our first nonregulated products was a home Internet service called Speedy. This was a new technology for us, and Speedy had some growing pains. In anticipation of these problems, we had created a consumer helpline where customers could call and get assistance with Speedy. Unknown to me at the time, we had also set up a second helpline for senior managers at Telesp—where senior managers could get the "extra help" that they might need to make Speedy work.

As soon as I found out about this second helpline, I closed it. If senior managers had difficulties with Speedy, they would have to get the same support as regular customers.

In the meantime, I signed up for the Speedy service myself and encountered some difficulties. So I called the helpline. The young man on the other end of the line was helpful and tried very hard, but after two hours, he still couldn't make Speedy work for me.

Finally, I told him, "I just want to let you know that I am the CEO of Telesp, and that I have been very impressed by your effort to fix my problems."

He didn't believe me.

It took a while, but I finally convinced him that I was the CEO. Then I asked, "What kind of support from Telesp would you need to have been able to address my problem?"

This 19-year-old young man articulately described 14 things he would need to have to be able to address my problems. I said, "You sound like you know a great deal about how to fix problems with Speedy. Would you be willing to come to our next corporate executive committee meeting and share the list you have just shared with me?"

It took some convincing, but he finally agreed. Two weeks later, this young man—an hourly employee at our call center affiliate—gave a presentation to the executive committee about the 14 things we needed to do in order to help Speedy customers use this product. I thanked him and asked him to leave the meeting.

I then turned to the senior manager in charge of Speedy and asked, "How many of these 14 issues did you know about?" He responded, "About half." I then turned to the rest of the executive team. "As of today, we are suspending sales of Speedy. We are not going to continue to sell a product that we do not know how to support. Also, I expect that at our next meeting, the Speedy team will present a plan for how we are going to fix the 14 problems that need to be solved to help our customers. When that plan is implemented, we will begin selling Speedy again. And I am going to invite the young man you have just seen—and some of his call center colleagues—to be at this next meeting to make sure that the plan you propose will address the issues he has raised."

Two weeks later, a plan was presented. Shortly thereafter, it was fully implemented and we started selling Speedy again. I hired the young man from the call center into a management trainee job in the firm, and Speedy became a very successful product.

This is a great story. It has all the critical elements of a good story—a setting, characters, plot, conflict, and resolution. Indeed, it is almost a prototypical "rags to riches" story of a young man plucked from the obscurity of a call center to teach the organization's elite a little about what really goes on in the company.[12] It is entertaining. It is inspiring. It almost feels like it could be an outline for a movie script.

But this story was much more. It began the process of changing the culture at Telesp. This story was told and retold throughout the company. Ultimately, it was picked up by the leading business magazine in Brazil and printed as a lead article. And every time it was told, and retold, it sent a clear message to those who worked at Telesp: "The old command-and-control culture at Telesp is dead. We are developing a new culture where we must all work together to serve our customers." It gave employees—people who had for years never been asked how the firm's operations could be improved—hope that their ideas might actually be listened to.

And it wasn't just this story that had impact. This story started a "story cascade"—where people throughout the organization began to feel empowered to rethink the culture in the part of the business where they worked. And as they did so, they built their own stories, which led to other stories, and so on. Also, Manoel did not stop with this one story—he built others that all reinforced a simple message: "The old Telesp culture is gone; the new employee-engaged and customer-focused culture at Telesp is here."

And Telesp's culture changed. The organization was transformed. As a result, it was not only able to weather the storm created by new competition and new telecom technologies, it thrived in that storm. It became the most successful telecom company in Brazil, while the performance of telecom firms that maintained their command-and-control cultures faltered.

Also, note what the beginning of this culture-change process did *not* include: a well-defined list of values that the leader wanted the new culture to have, a plan for numerous training programs on what these values were and how they were to be implemented, and various kinds of incentives consistent with these new values. Some of these programs and policies came later,[13] but only after the leader showed, through his own actions, that he was irreversibly committed to culture change.

Building a Culture-Changing Story Database

While the story of Manoel at Telesp is interesting, it is just one example. There are already other examples of this kind of story building in the literature. If we were going to be able to document the effect of building stories on culture change that generalized beyond a few special cases, we needed to build a much broader database of such stories. So that is what we did.

The database we built includes over 150 stories derived from interviews with over 50 business leaders. These leaders included many CEOs—like Manoel Amorim—in both large and medium-sized firms. However, it also included division general managers in large global corporations; leaders in sales, manufacturing, supply chain, and other functions in large and medium-sized companies; plant managers; entrepreneurs in small firms; college deans in universities; and so forth.

Some of the leaders we interviewed perceived a mismatch between their organization's culture and the strategies they wanted to pursue and built stories that changed their culture to align with these strategies. Others did not think that such a mismatch existed or tried to change their cultures without building stories. Still others tried to change their cultures by building stories but failed in this effort. This variance in outcomes in our sample made it possible to identify the kinds of stories business leaders need to build in order to change their cultures.[14] Those results are presented in this book.

The Attributes of Successful Culture-Changing Stories

The six attributes of stories built by business leaders that are likely to change a firm's culture are presented in Table 1.1. How they were exemplified in the first story that Manoel Amorim built to change the culture at Telesp is briefly summarized here. Much of the rest of this book examines how the culture-changing stories built by different business leaders have incorporated these six attributes.

The Actions That Build These Stories Are Authentic

One of the biggest challenges in changing an organization's culture is that its employees and other stakeholders are often unsure about how committed a business leader is to culture change. Because of this, they will closely watch each of a leader's actions, and parse each of the leader's speeches, searching for the limits of their commitment to culture change. Employees and stakeholders that perceive a mismatch between your culture-change rhetoric and your actual behavior will often choose to "sit out" your culture-change efforts, knowing that these efforts are unlikely to be sustained.

TABLE 1.1 Attributes of Successful Culture-Changing Stories
1. The actions that build these stories are authentic.
2. These stories "star" the leader.
3. The actions that build these stories signal a clean break with the past, with a clear path to the future.
4. These stories appeal to employees' heads and hearts.
5. The actions that build these stories are often theatrical.
6. These stories are told and retold throughout an organization.

So, to be credible, the actions taken by leaders that build culture-changing stories must reflect their deepest personal convictions—about who they are as people, what they value most in an organization, and how they think about the relationship between an organization's culture and its ability to perform. In other words, to be successful, your commitment to culture change and the stories you build to facilitate this change must be authentic.

Fortunately, as we will describe in Chapter 3, you don't have to be perfect in modeling a new culture to lead culture change. In fact, sometimes your failure to live up to your own highest values can be a source of a culture-changing story.

However, while you may sometimes fall short of living your own values, your employees must nevertheless believe that—at your core—you are committed to culture change. This means that the stories you build to change your organization's culture must be authentic to who you are, what you value, and how you think culture and strategy are linked.

Not surprisingly, as we will see in Chapter 3, this kind of story building almost always increases your personal vulnerability in your organization.

Thus, before building a story to begin the process of changing the culture at Telesp, Manoel had to be certain that a nonhierarchical customer service–oriented culture was going to be a competitive necessity for his firm. He had to be certain that he was willing to have the difficult conversations needed with his subordinates in order to make this kind of culture change happen. He had to be comfortable with the fact that some of his employees— even some of his best-performing employees (in the old culture)—might have to be let go as part of this culture change. And he had to be comfortable with committing to changing his firm's culture before the limitations of its current culture were fully manifest, even while knowing that the performance benefits of the new culture he was trying to build might not materialize for some time.

If Manoel was not fully comfortable with these and other implications of changing Telesp's culture, then there would always be a chance that he would not remain committed to culture change, especially if that change took longer or faced stronger headwinds than expected. Employees could have spotted this ambiguous commitment to culture change, and simply waited until Manoel's "fake commitment" waned and the old culture reasserted itself.

Since Manoel's commitment to culture change was authentic, the stories he built to facilitate culture change were accepted as authentic by his employees and other stakeholders.

A Successful Culture-Changing Story "Stars" the Leader

We have already suggested that stories about famous athletes, self-sacrificing politicians, and bootstrapping entrepreneurs can be interesting and motivating. But culture-changing stories are not about someone else. They are about you—the business leader. If you are going to build stories to change your organizational culture, *you* have to "star" in these stories. The only way that the stories you build can reveal your irreversible commitment to culture change is if your actions are central to building these stories.

This doesn't mean that you are the only player in your stories. The best story builders often involve other employees as participants or observers to witness those stories being built. This facilitates the communication of a story throughout your firm. It also helps create the "story cascade" mentioned earlier by enabling these and other members of your organization to build their own stories.

While Manoel was not the only "star" in the story he built, he was the major actor. Without his actions, there would have been no story, and without this story, there may well not have been the required culture change. But Manoel was not alone when he built these stories—some of its key elements took place in executive team meetings. This helped create a story cascade within Telesp that was instrumental in changing the organization's culture.

The Actions That Build a Story Establish a Clean Break with the Past Along with a Clear Path to the Future

Culture change is not "business as usual." In fact, it's about "no longer business as usual." So the story you build has to be based on actions you take that clearly violate the values, beliefs, and norms that currently dominate your organization's culture. These actions must be intentionally, even emphatically, radical.

Your actions also have to create a clear path forward. That path does not have to be detailed—in fact, as will be shown later (in Chapter 9), having a too detailed vision of the future culture in a firm can actually make it difficult to realize that future culture. Force-feeding a new culture down your employees' throats will often not lead to culture change. But your story does have to show a path forward to a new culture that will differ in some important ways from the current culture.

For these reasons, rarely will it be the case that a single story built by a business leader will be enough to change a culture—especially if that culture is deeply entrenched. So not only does your first story have to create a clear break with the past and a path to the future, so do your second, and third, and fourth, and the many more stories you build.

The timing of your first story is also critical. You may have heard the phrase "If it ain't broke, don't fix it." But if you wait to build your first culture-changing story until your culture's impact on your performance is broken, it may be too late to change your culture. Organizational cultures, and their relationship to your firm's performance, need to be constantly evaluated and, as appropriate, adjusted. The stories you build will help you accomplish this objective.

Manoel had become CEO of a very centralized, very hierarchical—and yet very successful—organization. He had to show that the old culture which had emphasized top-down decision making to address performance goals imposed on it by the government would have to be replaced with a collaborative culture that focused on satisfying customers. And he had to do this before the hierarchical culture began preventing the firm from addressing the needs of new customers. He did this by asking hourly employees to present their analysis of their company's problems to the most senior managers in the firm—essentially turning Telesp's culture upside down. This was a break with the past with a path toward a new cultural future.

These Stories Appeal to Your Employees' Heads and Hearts

A culture-changing story must demonstrate a clear connection between a new culture and the financial performance of your firm. It must be built on the assumption that culture change is not a passing fancy but is a rational, hard-nosed requirement for a firm's survival and economic success. That is, culture-changing stories must appeal to your employees' heads. But because changing culture is also about changing the way employees and other stakeholders feel and think, a culture-changing story must also appeal to their hearts—to their emotions, to their highest values, to what Abraham Lincoln called the "better angels of our nature." In this way, your efforts to change a culture must not be just a purely economic play, they must also be a call for your employees to join in a noble enterprise.

Manoel's analysis of competition in a deregulated environment provided compelling logic that there was a fundamental mismatch between this firm's old culture and its new competitive realities—an argument that appealed to the head. By choosing an "underdog" employee to lead a customer-service revolution, Manoel was also appealing to the heart of his employees.

The Actions That Build a Successful Culture-Changing Story Are Often Theatrical

These stories are entertaining. They are dramatic—they have good guys and bad guys. The actions used to build these stories are sufficiently striking that the stories will be repeatedly discussed around the real and electronic watercoolers in the firm—just like a good movie or game gets discussed. Building stories often involves business leaders doing things that "business leaders in the company are just not supposed to do," or at least what prior leaders would never have done—dressing up in costumes, singing songs, acting in comedic plays, and so forth. And for these reasons, it is personally risky.

Sometimes a business leader can feel pretty foolish getting involved in these theatrical efforts. But this is theater with purpose—to exemplify a new culture in a public and engaging way. It also sends a message about just how seriously a leader is committed to culture change.

Manoel built a classic "rags to riches" story—a story genre that has enduring popularity. Whether it be Pip becoming a wealthy gentleman in the Dickens classic *Great Expectations*, or Rocky Balboa leaving the slums of Philadelphia to become heavyweight champion of the world in *Rocky*, or an operator at a call center teaching the senior executives at Telesp how to fix product problems, it's all the same. But stories like the one Manoel built are even more powerful, because they are true. And in this case, it all began with the CEO staying on the phone for over two hours trying to solve a technology product problem—a very "non-CEO-like thing to do."

The Stories Are Told and Retold in an Organization

Culture change is not done in private and in back rooms. It engages most of a firm's employees and other stakeholders. And so, stories that are built to facilitate cultural change must also be public. Great culture-changing stories are retold frequently, and thoughtful leaders will find many opportunities and venues to retell these stories.

Retelling these stories also enables your employees to build their own stories. This helps create the story cascade that ultimately will help transform your culture.

Manoel's story was built in the company's executive committee—a public venue—and news about this event spread like wildfire. Later, it was distributed in the firm's internal newsletter. Moreover, the outcomes of this story—a revision of the customer support function—were also very public. Later, this story became the lead article in Brazil's most important business magazine—so not only did Telesp's employees know about it, all of the firm's other stakeholders did as well.[15]

Our research shows that these six characteristics of culture-changing stories dramatically increased the probability that the business leaders who built them were able to lead their organizations through a culture change. In fact, most of the successful culture-changing stories we have identified have most, if not all, of these attributes.

Is Culture Change Important Just for CEOs?

Clearly, the answer to this question is NO! Culture mediates the relationship between your strategies and your organization's performance. Your strategies are the bundle of activities your organization engages in to gain competitive advantages. To do this, these activities must increase your organization's revenues and/or reduce its costs, and must do so in a way that current and potential competitors find costly to imitate.[16]

However, these strategic activities can exist at multiple levels in your organization. So, for example, a CEO may seek a competitive advantage by engaging in activities that differentiate the organization's products relative to competitors' products. Functional business leaders and plant or office managers can engage in such activities when they implement quality manufacturing processes, when they develop marketing campaigns, when they develop training programs, and so forth. And business leaders deeper within an organization can engage in strategic activities when they co-operate to improve organizational processes and practices of all kinds.

In short, strategy and competitive advantage are way too important to be left with just the CEO and other top managers. In the best firms, strategy and competitive advantage are every business leader's responsibility.

Thus, since every business leader in an organization can engage in activities that have strategic implications, it follows that every business leader needs to be concerned with how the culture in the part of the organization where they lead aligns with the strategies they are pursuing to help create competitive advantage. If there is a misalignment, then these business leaders will need to change their culture—and the story-building techniques discussed in this book are directly relevant.

Does Culture Change Apply Only to For-Profit Organizations?

The answer to this question is also clearly NO! To the extent that an organization—for-profit, not-for-profit, NGO, governmental agency, and so forth—has some set of goals or objectives it is trying to accomplish, then culture change may be important to leaders within that organization.

This will be the case when the actions you want to take to improve your organization's performance are not aligned with its culture. In these settings, whether you are working in a for-profit or not-for-profit setting, you will need to change your culture, and the story-building tools discussed in this book will help you accomplish this.

A Book on Culture Change, Not a Book on an Ideal Culture

Before presenting the results of our research in more detail, it is important for you to understand one way that this book differs from most prior books on organizational culture and firm performance. Most of these books have attempted to identify some sort of ideal organizational culture to which most, if not all, firms should aspire. Implicitly, these books have invited you to compare your culture with this ideal and to change your culture as needed.

This focus on identifying an ideal culture goes back to the very beginning of work on the relationships among organizational culture, firm strategies, and firm performance cited at the beginning of this chapter. While
acknowledging the importance of this previous work, this book is *not* about
describing such an ideal organizational culture. It seems to us that what
makes an organizational culture ideal depends on how it aligns with the
strategies that the firm is implementing. Different strategies will require different cultures for implementation. Thus, to the extent that firms pursue
different strategies, it is unlikely that there is one ideal culture to which all
organizations should aspire.

Instead, this book is about how you can change your organizational culture when it is misaligned with your strategy. We have studied firms that
have successfully changed their cultures from being deeply hierarchical in
nature to being much more participative, and vice versa. We have studied
firms that have changed their cultures from technology driven to consumer
driven, and vice versa. We have studied firms that have changed their cultures from emphasizing low cost and efficiency to emphasizing product differentiation and innovation, and vice versa. The point is that this is not a
book that identifies some ideal culture for your firm. It is a book about how
to change your culture so that it aligns with your strategy, no matter what
those changes are substantively.[17]

Our main assumptions in doing this work have been that you, a leader
in your organization, are best positioned to know (1) the strategies you need
to pursue to enhance the performance of your organization, (2) the kind of
culture you will need to realize the full potential of these strategies, and (3)
whether or not your current culture will need to be changed to align with
these strategies. Our task is to help you build stories to change your culture if that is necessary.

Our Methodology

The six attributes of effective culture-changing stories were developed
through an analysis of over 150 culture-changing stories obtained from over
50 interviews conducted over 18 months. These interviews were conducted
with a variety of different types of business leaders—including presidents,
CEOs, functional vice presidents, entrepreneurial founders, and so forth—
some of whom attempted to change their organizational cultures.

As suggested earlier, not all the business leaders we interviewed for this study tried to change their organizational cultures. Moreover, not all those who did try to change their organizational cultures, built stories to do so. And not all those leaders who did try to change their cultures by building stories were successful in changing their cultures. In short, our data collection did not examine only cases where leaders successfully built stories to change their cultures. This made it possible for us to identify the attributes of stories that are positively correlated with successful culture change.

The business leaders we interviewed were identified in three ways. First, all three authors have long histories of working with business leaders, working at many different levels in organizations, and working in a wide variety of industries around the globe. Many of these leaders were contacted and asked if they would be willing to be interviewed. Second, two of the authors (Manoel Amorim and Carlos Júlio) are members of the Young Presidents' Organization (YPO) and invited many of their contacts in that organization to be interviewed. Third, Manoel Amorim is a member of the Marriott School of Business National Advisory Committee and the Harvard Business School Alumni Group, both of which were sources of interviews. When invited, people were told that the topic of the interview would be to discuss how they, as business leaders, had attempted to change their organizational cultures.

Interviews were conducted via Zoom and typically lasted one hour. The purpose of the study was reiterated, and interviewees were asked if they would be willing to have their name and the name of their company revealed in the book. Most of those interviewed agreed to reveal their and their company's name, although there were sometimes specific facts that emerged in an interview that we were asked to not share. We have honored those requests and the few additional requests for anonymity.[18]

The interviews were recorded, and transcripts were created. These transcriptions were then organized into different culture-changing stories that a particular leader had built over his or her career. On average, leaders who built stories to try to change their organization's cultures shared around four stories each.

The six attributes of effective culture-changing stories were developed by analyzing approximately half of the stories in the database. These categories were then used to analyze the second half of the interviews in the database, as a way to test the generalizability of our list of attributes. Some of the stories in the database did not possess more than one or two of the story attributes identified. Some of these "miscellaneous" stories were very interesting but did not contribute to our broader understanding of the culture-change process. Also, not all the stories that had five or six of these attributes led to successful culture change. But the preponderance of the evidence in our analysis was consistent with the idea that these six story attributes contributed to successful culture change.

We made no attempt to verify the facts in these stories. These kinds of stories get told and retold in organizations, and often change with each retelling. We quickly concluded that efforts to objectively find out what was actually done to build a story in a firm would be futile. This was exemplified by one of the stories that came from our interviews:

STORY 1.2 "Was It Cheese or a Doughnut?"
Andy Theurer as CEO at ARUP Laboratories

When I was CFO of ARUP, I established a zero-tolerance policy for dishonesty and fraud. Given that we are in the medical lab testing business, our ability to conduct accurate and timely tests in a safe and ethical manner, while maintaining the confidentiality of our clients, was essential. Dishonesty and fraud were unacceptable in this setting.

One of the first times this issue came up was years ago, when an employee told me the following story. She had brought a bag of string cheese into the office, put it in the refrigerator in the break room, and when she came back to get the cheese, it was gone. Some days later, she brought another bag of string cheese—I guess she liked string cheese—to the office, put it in the common refrigerator, came back, and—once again—it was gone. She did this a third time with exactly the same result. Apparently, someone was stealing her cheese!

We decided to install a very simple camera in the break room to see who might be doing this. So, after installing the camera, she brought in another bag of string cheese and, as if on cue, it was stolen. However, this time we had video evidence about who stole her cheese. It was someone who worked in IT.

I called the culprit into my office, told him about the cheese being stolen, and gave him every opportunity to confess. He didn't. Then I told him that we had video evidence about who had stolen the cheese, and still he didn't confess. Finally, I showed him the video, and he remained silent.

I immediately fired him for cause—not because stealing string cheese was such a huge deal, but because we needed a zero-tolerance policy on unethical behavior in the company, and because he wouldn't own up to his mistakes. We couldn't tolerate this kind of behavior.

Later, we found out that he had been stealing laptop computers from the lab and selling them. So, the cheese-stealing incident was only the tip of the iceberg. But through this story, I became known for my intolerance toward dishonest or unethical behavior in the company.

Funny thing, though. Many years later, after I became CEO, one of my direct reports told me how he came to know that I had zero tolerance for dishonesty or unethical behavior in the company. He told me that he had heard that I had fired someone, on the spot, for taking a doughnut out of a box of doughnuts left on a counter in the break room.

I had to laugh out loud. How the story about someone repeatedly stealing string cheese—and laptop computers—morphed into a story about someone taking a doughnut, I'll never know. And while it is very unlikely that I would ever fire someone for taking a doughnut from a box left on a counter in the break room, both stories—the cheese story and the doughnut story—communicate a core organizational value that is still important at ARUP: we are 100 percent committed to honesty and ethical behavior.

Thus, the point of these stories is not what did or did not actually happen when a story was built, but what the implications of these stories were for changing a firm's culture. In this sense, the stories in our database can be thought of as organizational myths in the way that anthropologists use the term "myth": Whether or not they reflect what actually went on in an organization, the messages they send about what values, beliefs, and norms should be dominant in a new culture are what is most important about these stories.[19]

We have no doubt that the results of these interviews, including evaluations of whether or not culture change actually occurred in an organization, reflect the preferences and biases of the individual leaders we interviewed. However, the pattern of our results across multiple interviews and multiple stories gives us confidence in our conclusions, despite these individual preferences and biases.

To make the stories printed in the book more readable, they were heavily edited from how they were given to us in the interviews. As a matter of courtesy, we passed these edited versions of the stories by the leaders who told them to us. We asked these individuals to ensure that the essential facts in a story were consistent with what they had told us. This led to a few minor edits of the stories, but in general the leaders we interviewed were willing to have their stories retold, warts and all, to help others learn how to lead cultural change in their own organizations.

Finally, not all the stories we collected and analyzed are included in the book. There were simply too many stories to include. However, all the stories we collected did have a substantive impact on the list of the six attributes of successful culture-changing stories we developed, and thus were essential to our research process.

CHAPTER TWO

Why Culture Change Is Different

C hange management is one of the most important responsibilities of leaders in modern organizations. Thus, it is not surprising that the process of managing organizational change has been widely studied, documented, and described. Based on this extensive work, a wide variety of models that describe how to successfully implement organizational change have been developed.

Here's the trick with these different models of how to successfully manage organizational change: They often don't agree with each other.

For example, some change models see organizational change as mostly a top-down process—that to be successful, change must start with a powerful or charismatic business leader with a clear vision of what changes need to be made and enough influence to make them. Other change models see organizational change as mostly a bottom-up or "grassroots" process—that to be successful, change must start either with individual employees evaluating and changing themselves, or with smaller groups within an organization changing how they act and what they value. In this model, organizational change occurs when these individual and small group changes accumulate to the point that they alter what an organization as a whole values and how it behaves.[1]

Other change models see organizational change as mostly a personal and deeply emotional process—that successful change necessarily involves altering how those involved with a firm feel about themselves and their interactions with the firm. In this model, organizational change is tracked by, among other things, changes in how emotionally engaged employees are with their firm. Still other change models see organizational change as mostly a logical and rational process—that successful change requires effective communication about what problems exist, why these problems are important for a firm's performance, how proposed solutions will address these problems, and so forth. In these models, how employees *feel* about a change is less important than their conclusions about whether or not a proposed solution will actually address important organizational problems.[2]

Finally, other change models focus neither on the vertical dimensions of the change process (is it more top-down or bottom-up?) nor on the affective dimensions to this process (does it focus more on employees' feelings or more on their rational conclusions?). These models instead focus on the need to align multiple attributes of an organization so that collectively they enable a firm to be effective in accomplishing its objectives. Different "systems" models of change management identify different organizational elements that need to be coordinated to generate organizational effectiveness. And these elements can be at the organizational or individual level. But the essential point of these change models is that organizations must be thought of as systems, and it is not possible to change one part of a system as if it were isolated from other parts of that system.[3]

It is likely that all of these models of how to effectively manage organizational change have some truth to them. Perhaps they each apply in different settings, to different kinds of organizational changes. Maybe ongoing research will help identify these settings, and conflicts among these different models can be resolved.

Or maybe not.

In any case, our research approach to understanding how you can change your organizational culture was not married to any one of these change management models. Our purpose was not to test one model against another model. Instead, we simply asked a group of business leaders how they tried to change their cultures.

And, from the point of view of the processes through which they tried to change their cultures, what we found is that successful culture change almost always applied multiple organizational change models—even when those models appeared to contradict each other. What we found is that culture-change management is both top-down and bottom-up. It focuses both on emotions and rationality. It focuses on individual and organizational systems. And sometimes it implements these seemingly contradictory features of change management at exactly the same time.

We call this approach to change management an *eclectic model of organizational change*. The business leaders we talked to adopted this eclectic approach to managing culture change because they thought that changing their culture required them to do so. In particular, they concluded that there were some characteristics of changing an organization's culture that made it impractical to apply just one model or approach to change. So they applied elements of a wide range of change management models.[4]

Indeed, our research suggested that business leaders who focused on using only one process to change their organizational cultures—say, top-down or bottom-up but not both—tended to be less successful in making these changes than those who took an eclectic approach. Moreover, these adverse outcomes didn't depend on which change model they happened to emphasize. No matter if they focused only on top-down or bottom-up change, or if they focused only on the emotional or the rational dimensions of change, or if they only focused on the systemic nature of culture change— in all these cases, efforts that applied a single model of organizational change were less effective than culture-change efforts that applied elements of multiple organizational change models.

Why Culture Change Requires an Eclectic Approach to Change Management

So, what is it about changing your organization's culture that requires an eclectic approach to change management? Our research suggests five attributes of culture—summarized in Table 2.1—that make the application of any one approach to change management likely to be less effective.

Culture Is Diffused throughout an Organization

First, organizational cultures are typically diffused widely throughout an organization. Thus, the answer to the question "who is responsible for an organization's culture?" is usually that *everyone* in a firm is responsible for

TABLE 2.1 Why Culture Change Requires an Eclectic Approach to Change
1. Culture is diffused throughout an organization.
2. Culture is an intangible asset.
3. Culture change threatens the status quo.
4. Culture change is both fast and slow.
5. Culture change can test the commitment of business leaders.

its culture. An organization's culture rarely resides in the mind of a single person or within a small group of influential managers. Rather, it is shared among many, if not most, of your employees. It is part of your firm's collective identity and thus is a shared asset. Indeed, one reason your culture can have such a profound impact on your ability to implement your strategies is precisely because it is so widely shared among your employees.

But when everyone is responsible for your organization's culture, then no one is responsible for your culture. When you have a problem with manufacturing quality in your company, you know who to call—the VP of manufacturing. If you aren't getting the kind of product recognition you need in the marketplace, you call the VP of marketing. If you can't hire the kind of employees you want, you know who is responsible for addressing this issue—the VP of human resources. But who do you call when you have to change your culture so you can more effectively implement your strategies? Ghostbusters?[5]

Perhaps some business leaders think they are responsible for their organization's culture. And certainly, you—as a business leader—can have an important impact on your firm's culture and how it evolves. In this sense, efforts to change a culture—because they often start with business leaders—are definitely top-down in nature.

However, if your organization's culture remains exclusively "yours" and is not diffused among your employees, it will have a limited impact on your firm's ability to implement its strategies. You must find ways to enroll your employees in the culture-change process so that they understand and appreciate the new culture, and are able to use it to help implement your strategies. In this sense, efforts to change your culture are not just top-down, they are equally bottom-up in nature.

In our research, we found that many business leaders started the culture-change process top-down but purposely left many of the details of culture change open—including the exact nature of the culture that they wanted to create. Instead, these business leaders invited their employees to cocreate this new culture with them—a process that had a decidedly bottom-up or grassroots feel. Indeed, as we will see, one way you can know that your top-down culture-change effort is being successful is when it starts being bottom-up in nature.

Thus, because you, as a business leader, can start and have an important impact on culture change in your organization, the culture-change process must be top-down. However, because your employees must cocreate this new culture with you, the culture-change process must also be bottom-up. A change model that is either top-down *or* bottom-up seems less likely to be successful in changing an organization's culture.

Culture Is an Intangible Asset

Second, unlike many other resources that are important for your company's financial success, organizational culture is an intangible asset. It is the values, norms, and beliefs that guide employee behavior when formal rules and policies do not exist or fail to give guidance. Thus, an organizational culture is a social construct—culture is real in its effects but exists mostly in the minds and thoughts of your employees.[6] While your culture can have a profound effect on the ability of your firm to implement its strategies, it is nevertheless an "invisible asset."[7]

Since culture is in the minds and thoughts of your employees, it is not surprising that changing culture usually involves changing the minds and thoughts of your employees. In this way, culture change can alter your employees' most cherished beliefs and values about working in your firm—how they identify with your company, their sense of engagement, even their loyalty to you as a business leader and to your firm as a collective. These are all deeply emotional and personal dimensions of organizational change and suggest that culture-change processes must appeal to your employees' hearts.

And yet, at the same time, changing this "invisible asset" may be vital in your ability to implement your business strategies. And the successful implementation of your strategies is essential if your firm is to generate competitive advantages. The links among culture, strategy implementation, competitive advantage, and firm performance are decidedly rational and profit-generating in orientation. Culture change that appeals only to your employees' hearts does not hold the promise of economic growth, job stability, or enhanced career opportunities as culture change that also appeals to your employees' heads.

Thus, as suggested in Chapter 6, successful culture change will need to have an impact on both your employees' emotions and feelings about your company, and your ability to generate competitive advantages from implementing your strategies. Thus, it must appeal to both your employees' hearts and heads. Change management approaches that appeal only to your employees' emotions and feelings, *or* only to their rational profit-maximizing selves, are less likely to be successful in changing your organization's culture.

Culture Change Threatens the Status Quo

Third, changing your organization's culture often has the effect of upending many established practices and policies associated with your old culture. "Winners" in the old culture might become "losers" in the new culture; people who were on the "outside" of the old culture may be central and on the "inside" in the new culture. People who were your close friends and allies in the old culture may become mere acquaintances or even adversaries in the new culture. In this sense, culture change "flips the script" that your employees have known and used in your organization.

Prior research suggests that most people don't like any kind of change—especially change that can affect their own status and the status of their friends in an organization. This kind of change creates fear. Even people who like change don't like changing that they like change.[8] And almost every organizational change disrupts the status quo and forces people to alter their understanding of how their work environment functions. And thus, almost every organizational change will be resisted by at least some of your employees.

But changing your organization's culture takes this resistance and puts it on steroids! Culture change is not just about changing work practices and policies—although changing these economically rational dimensions of an organization can be scary enough for some employees. It can also be about changing your company's identity and purpose, and thus the way that your employees emotionally engage with your firm. Change that not only threatens the *way* that you do your work but also *why* you do your work is more likely to be resisted than almost any other kind of organizational change.

Thus, to change an organization's culture, you need an approach to change that recognizes that resistance to change has both personal and emotional roots, as well as rational and economic roots. Adopting a change management model that does not enable you to respond to both these sources of resistance to change is less likely to be successful.

Culture Change Is Both Fast and Slow

Some organizational changes—approving a budget, promoting an employee, altering an HR policy—can happen quickly. Others—building a new plant, adjusting your supply chain, rebranding a product—can take longer.

However, changing your organization's culture is often both fast *and* slow. This creates unusual challenges when you are trying to manage culture change.

Culture change can be fast when certain parts of your organization— for example, a particular office or plant or work group—are able to change their culture quickly. Business leaders in these parts of your organization sometimes are able to communicate their cultural vision and to enlist the help of their employees to cocreate this new culture more efficiently than in your organization as a whole. These kinds of bottom-up changes can give your culture-change efforts a series of quick wins and can create a sense of momentum in changing the overall culture of your firm.

However, these kinds of quick wins often need to be coupled with the "slow wins" of changing an organization's overall culture if they are to lead to real change. Consider the experience of Frank Pipp, an assembly plant manager for a Ford Motor Company factory in the late 1960s. Pipp instructed his staff to purchase a Toyota pickup truck that his final assembly team could disassemble and then reassemble to learn firsthand about the quality of the final assembly of this Toyota product.

At Ford, if two connecting parts could be assembled without the use of a rubber mallet, they were said to "snap fit." Snap fit was the gold standard for assembling automobiles at the time. To Pipp's amazement, when the Toyota truck they had disassembled was reassembled, 100 percent of its parts were snap fit. He didn't believe this was possible, so he had his team repeat the exercise. They came to the same conclusion—100 percent of the Toyota parts were snap fit.

Pipp instantly understood the importance of these results for the quality of Ford's products, compared to Toyota. So he invited several important members of Ford's top management team to his plant, where he had his team demonstrate the quality of the Toyota's final assembly. According to Pipp, this is what happened next:

> Everyone was quiet, until the division general manager cleared his throat, and remarked, "The customer will never notice." And then everyone excitedly nodded in assent and exclaimed, "Yeah, yeah, that's right. The customer will never notice." And they all trotted off happy.[9]

Obviously, Pipp was on the verge of creating a cultural transformation in his assembly plant—a small culture-change win that could have had a significant impact on the culture of quality at Ford. But that potential was lost when a division general manager dismissed his work with "The customer will never notice."

We know now, of course, that this division general manager was wrong—the customer really did notice. However, it took many small culture wins, and many heroic efforts by plant managers over many years, until finally, in 1981—some 20 years later—Ford finally accepted that building a culture of quality needed to be its first priority and used this commitment as a marketing tagline: "At Ford, Quality Is Job 1." Even more recently, Ford has had to continue to develop its commitment to creating and maintaining a culture of quality.[10]

The Ford example shows both that quick wins can be important in changing an organization's overall culture, and that changing this overall culture can, nevertheless, be a slow process. This is especially true for organizations as large and complex as Ford Motor Company. As a business leader, you may have a clear idea of how you want your company's culture to change. But getting everyone aligned and on board with what you want your culture to be, and why you want it to be this way, can be very time consuming.

Of course, the slow pace of changing an organization's overall culture can test the patience of even the most patient business leader. And yet, until the overall culture in your firm changes, quick culture-change wins within your company are at risk of being only short-lived experiments. Like weeds in a garden, these quick wins can burst through fertile ground with enthusiasm, only to be plucked by an all-powerful "gardener"—your firm's well-established culture.

Indeed, the cultural entrepreneurs within your firm who are creating these quick culture-change wins may unknowingly be taking significant personal risks if they move out ahead in culture change, beyond where others in your company are comfortable. While you may be enthusiastic about these quick wins, others in your firm may look at them with suspicion and distrust. In this setting, what started out as quick wins may turn into painful defeats or merely "interesting experiments" as bottom-up efforts to create culture change are ground down by the glacial pressure of a well-established corporate culture.

In one organization with which we are familiar, the manager of a small business unit helped implement a new and cooperative culture that led to the development of several new services. However, the broader organization within which this business was located was very hierarchical, almost dictatorial. This business unit manager's cultural experiments were seen by the broader organization as threatening the cultural status quo, and this business unit manager was ultimately dismissed—even though his operation was more successful, more innovative, and had higher employee engagement than had ever been the case previously.[11]

Thus, while quick wins are exciting and an important part of any culture-change process, they are often unsustainable without broader changes in your organizational culture. On the other hand, such broader organizational culture changes are not likely without at least some momentum-building quick wins.

It follows that change models that focus on creating quick wins *or* broader scale organizational change are less likely to be successful when applied to changing organizational culture than change models that recognize the importance of both fast *and* slow dimensions of culture change.

Culture Change Can Test the Commitment of Business Leaders

Taken together, these attributes of culture suggest that culture change will often be challenging and difficult. Culture change is usually not about efficiently applying a single model of organizational change. It is more often about combining multiple models of change in a complex and constantly evolving way. It is operating in both top-down and bottom-up processes, appealing to both your employees' hearts and their heads, and moving both fast and slow as you create quick culture-change wins within your company while also trying to alter your firm's overall culture.

Yikes! No wonder culture change often fails.[12]

Many of these challenges emerge because culture is a complex system of interrelated elements. These elements of your organization's culture include your personal values and beliefs, the diverse values and beliefs of your employees, your organization's strategies, its formal structure, its social norms, its formal policies and practices, its history, and so forth. Changing any one element of this cultural system can create conflict with other elements of this system. On the other hand, changing all these cultural elements at once is also challenging.

Given the complexity of this change process, it is not unreasonable to expect that a business leader's commitment to culture change can vary over time. In the early days of culture change, leaders can voice their commitment to creating a new culture, can fund culture training and other change initiatives, and can create a wide variety of culture-change task forces. But all of this is what economists call "cheap talk."[13] Employees throughout the firm know—or at least suspect—that their leader's commitment to creating a new culture can change suddenly, and dramatically so.

For example, leaders can sound very committed to changing a firm's culture—until there is a problem with a firm's financial performance. Then it's "all hands on deck" to improve the numbers, regardless of the impact of these actions on culture change. At the very least, when financial performance is in doubt, everyone knows—or at least suspects—that culture change is going to drop down on the leader's priority list.

Employees also know—or at least suspect—that if culture change leads to situations that make the leader uncomfortable with a new culture, any commitment to the new values of a new culture can easily be reversed. This can even be the case if the business leader was instrumental in creating the new values of the new culture. If you begin to feel vulnerable about a culture change, or uncertain whether you can authentically continue to support such a change, then it is likely that your employees will know—or at least suspect—that your commitment to culture change may not be reliable.

When employees believe that the commitment of a firm's leaders to culture change is just so much "cheap talk," employees know—or at least suspect—that such efforts will not be successful. Of course, they will play the game, go to the training, sign the commitments, and do all the other things that are the artifacts of traditional culture change. They do so, knowing that—like kidney stones—"this too will pass." Given enough time, efforts to change the culture will dissipate and finally wither away, and the old culture will reemerge unchanged and perhaps even strengthened.

None of this suggests that what you say, as a business leader, is unimportant in changing an organization's culture. Indeed, your language can be very important in inspiring employees throughout your company to become part of the culture-change process. Your words are an important way that you can begin to connect to the hearts of your employees.

But a change management model that focuses only on the words you say will usually not be successful—by itself. Your words are only one part of changing the complex system that is culture change. Thus, in addition to your words, you need to apply a change management model that recognizes all these elements of culture change, and reassures your employees that you are irreversibly committed to changing your organization's culture even when things get difficult and culture-change headwinds start to blow.

How Building Stories Facilitates Culture Change

Given the attributes of organizational cultures listed in Table 2.1, it wasn't surprising that our research found that business leaders—everyone from CEOs to business school deans to plant managers to project managers to entrepreneurs—were more successful in implementing culture change when they adopted elements of multiple organizational change models. Successful culture change is top-down and bottom-up, focuses on emotions and rational decision making, and is all about changing the cultural system in your company. It follows that successful culture change takes a more eclectic approach to change management.

However, in the midst of these eclectic approaches to culture change, our research found one remarkable point of consistency: no matter how these business leaders mixed and matched different models of organizational change, they almost all built stories as part of the culture-change process.

At one level, this makes perfect sense. As was suggested in Chapter 1, the mechanism through which cultures are diffused and maintained in an organization is through the stories your employees tell about your company, how it conducts business, what it values, and so forth. Stories are the lifeblood of your culture. It makes sense, then, that if you want to change your organizational culture, you need to change the stories that your employees tell each other.

Of course, not all stories you could build are equally successful in creating culture change. Our research identified six attributes of stories that increase the likelihood that they will change an organization's culture. These six story attributes were summarized in Chapter 1 and are discussed in more detail in the rest of this book.

But it also turns out that story building helps you address the challenges associated with changing an organization's culture, identified in Table 2.1. How story building does this is summarized in Table 2.2.

How Building Stories Addresses the "Diffused Culture" Problem

Yes, your organizational culture is diffused throughout your organization. But the stories you build, if they have the six attributes identified by our research, will cut a wide swath through your company. They will cut across boundaries between functional areas in your firm, and between your different businesses, plants, and locations—your marketing people in one division will share the same stories as your manufacturing people in another division. They will also transcend vertical distinctions in your firm—your top management team will share these stories right along with your hourly workers.

TABLE 2.2	How Building Stories Addresses the Challenges Associated with Culture Change (See Table 2.1)
Culture is diffused throughout your organization.	Well-formed stories cut across horizontal and vertical boundaries in your company, and can unite business leaders and employees in culture-change efforts.
Culture is an intangible asset.	Well-formed stories make intangible and invisible assets more tangible and visible.
Culture change threatens the status quo.	Well-formed stories identify culture-change heroes throughout an organization, which can inspire others to support culture change.
Culture change is fast and slow.	Slow culture-change stories can enable fast culture-change wins, while fast culture-change wins can enable more story building for overall culture change.
Culture change can test the commitment of business leaders.	Building authentic stories make it difficult for business leaders to back out of their changing commitments, but can also enable them to introduce those commitments gradually.

Indeed, it is the wide diffusion of these stories throughout your firm that is the process by which old culture-defining stories are replaced by new culture-defining stories.

In this way, building well-formed stories can help unite your entire company around culture change. These stories can help instill a sense of pride as your employees, at all levels and in all groups, share stories that exemplify a new culture that will help your organization implement its new strategies.

And here is what is most amazing about this process. If you build authentic stories in which you, the business leader, "star," and that have all the other attributes described in this book, then these stories will spread throughout your organization on their own.

For free!

Like wildfire!

This will happen almost automatically, as employees gather—either in the real world or online—to share what they have heard about what you have done.

Some of your employees will shake their heads in disbelief about the story or stories you have built. Others will question your sanity. Others will whisper, "It's about time." Still others will see you as your company's savior.

And some will build their own culture-changing stories.

Of course, you can augment this communication process by sharing the stories you have built through formal media in your company. You can even enlist media outside your company to help share these stories—the advantages and disadvantages of doing this are discussed in more detail in Chapter 8. Also, these stories can become an important part of the training that is part of your onboarding process.

But one reason that building well-formed stories is such an effective way of changing an organization's culture is that such stories diffuse every bit as broadly as your culture, and thus begin to replace your organization's old culture stories with new culture stories.

How Building Stories Addresses the "Intangible Asset" Problem

Yes, culture is an intangible asset. But stories your employees share about working in your firm can make your culture more tangible and more visible. Employees may not understand exactly what "think creatively" means in the abstract, but the story of how Post-it notes were developed at 3M exemplifies innovation at this firm.[14] Managers may not understand what "valuing employee teamwork" means in the abstract. But a story of how employees at Southwest Airlines—from hourly baggage handlers to pilots—work together to get luggage on an airplane takes this abstract idea and makes it real.[15] Salespeople may not understand what "world class customer service means" in the abstract, but when they hear a story of doing whatever it takes to satisfy a customer at Nordstrom's, they get it.[16]

In the same way, employees may not understand the kind of culture you are trying to create if the only way you communicate it is through lofty discussions of lists of company values. This is one reason why so many employees mock these lists when they are plastered on the walls of your firm.

But this is where the stories you build can be so helpful. They take the abstract and make it real. They take a possible future and make a path toward that future real. They take the intangible and invisible and make it tangible and visible. Employees at Telesp did not need to look to any list of values that defined a customer service–oriented culture. All they had to do was share the story of the call center employee.

How Building Stories Addresses the "Status Quo Bias" Problem

It is absolutely the case that building culture-changing stories can change the status quo in a firm. And those who have succeeded in the old culture may resist efforts to change to the new culture.

But recall that culture change in this context is not about changing an organization's cultural values for the sake of change. Nor is it about remaking a firm's culture in the likeness of a business leader. Indeed, if these are the motivations behind a business leader building culture-changing stories, then incumbent managers should resist these changes. And resist with energy.

However, if a firm needs to change its strategies to maintain or improve its performance, and if the implementation of these new strategies requires a new culture, then culture change is not optional. Indeed, it can be existential. Here, you actually have a responsibility to change the status quo.

In these settings, employees who build stories to help change a culture can be legitimately thought of as organizational heroes. Of course, the term "hero" is used so widely now that it has almost ceased to have meaning. But if a hero is an individual (or group) that does something that must be done (like changing an organization's culture so it can implement its strategies) and these actions are personally risky (as they often can be with respect to changing an organization's culture) then those people, in our minds, are heroes. A hero in the military puts his or her life at risk to save the lives of others; culture-change heroes put their careers at risk to help an organization survive and thrive.

Such heroic acts often inspire people in an organization to join in a culture-change effort, even if such changes might be difficult for them.

Of course, some of your employees may resist culture change, even in the face of heroic efforts by people in your organization. It may be a difficult choice for you, but such employees—especially if they are in visible and influential positions—usually cannot remain with your organization. This can be true even if these people have been among the best performers in the old culture and even if they are your close personal friends.

How Building Stories Addresses the "Fast and Slow" Problem

Story building works for both fast and slow culture change. As we've already suggested, our research shows that culture change often starts with the business leader in charge—the person who is best positioned to see the need to implement new strategies and the mismatch between these new strategies and an organization's current culture. But just announcing the need for a new culture, or developing lists of new cultural values, or any of these other purely top-down approaches to change are not likely to be successful in this context.

Instead, these business leaders build a story.

A well-formed story with the six characteristics described in this book will begin the overall organizational culture-change process. This is the slow part of culture change. But this initial story creates space for managers throughout an organization to build their own culture-changing stories. This is the fast part of culture change and is the story cascade process discussed briefly in Chapter 1, and in more detail in Chapter 8.

These fast culture-change wins, in turn, enable a business leader to build additional stories—either about these fast wins or completely new stories. Thus, building stories in the slow culture-change process enables building stories in the fast culture-change process, and building stories in the fast culture-change process can enable building additional stories in the slow process.

How Building Stories Addresses the "Business Leader Commitment" Problem

Finally, with each story you build, you send a message to your employees that your commitment to culture change is increasingly irreversible. Depending on the kind of stories you start building, your employees may be somewhat skeptical at first. But as your stories become more authentic, more personal, and more public, your commitment to culture change becomes more credible—despite the challenges that such change necessarily encounters. And this makes it more likely that at least some of your employees will get off the sidelines and actually help cocreate the culture with you.

In this sense, building culture-changing stories is a signal of just how committed you are to culture change in your organization.

If you are nervous about your ability to make a long-term commitment to culture change, then adopting a story-building approach to change has some obvious advantages. First and foremost, you don't have to commit to the entire culture-change process up front. All you need to do to start this process is to build your first story. Then see how it goes. If you follow the guidelines identified in this book, it will probably go pretty well. You will begin to find it easier to implement your strategies. And then you can build another story, and another story. After a while, your employees will gain confidence in your commitment to culture change. And then your employees will start building their own stories. As your culture begins to change, you can align the rest of your organization with this new culture. And, after some period of time, you will be able to look back and realize that you have cocreated a new culture with your employees.

Congratulations.

Culture Change, Not Culture Destruction

Of course, throughout this book, we are not talking about simply *destroying* your organization's culture. It is well known that it can take years for a culture to develop and mature in an organization, and that an unthinking business leader can destroy this culture in an afternoon. Rather, the culture change we are talking about is engaging in actions that modify—sometimes radically—a firm's existing culture to more fully align it with its strategies. This kind of culture change is purposeful and strategic. Yes, it may involve fundamentally changing an organization's values, beliefs, and norms, but it is not reckless in nature.

A US politician once observed that "any jackass can kick down a barn, but it takes a skilled carpenter to build one."[17] Many of the business leaders we studied were "skilled carpenters," whose medium of choice was building culture-changing stories that enabled their firms to more effectively implement their strategies.

Are You Ready for Culture Change?

So, here is what we have learned from our research. First, you *can* change your organization's culture, and this can enable you to more effectively implement your strategies. However, you can't change your culture by applying a single change management model—you need to adopt elements of many of these models. In other words, you don't need a change management hammer, or a change management screwdriver, you need an entire change management tool kit. Effective culture change is top-down and bottom-up, focuses on emotional and rational dimensions of change, and treats culture as a system of interrelated elements.

Second, as you adopt this eclectic approach to change management in trying to change your culture, the one element of culture change that seems to be constant is building stories—stories that are authentic, "star" you as the leader, create a break with the past and a path to the future, appeal to your employees' heads and hearts, are often theatrical, and are told and retold throughout your organization. Building these kinds of stories are at the core of successful culture change.

But as with any major change you might be contemplating, before you begin the culture-change process by building your first story, you need to be sure of two things. First, you must be certain that you *need* to change your culture. And second, you must be certain that you have the *will* necessary to change your culture.

You need to change your culture when doing so will enable you to more effectively implement your strategies. Any other motivation for changing your organization's culture—to leave a legacy, to satisfy your ego, or because you simply would prefer working in a different organizational culture—is not likely to be compelling for your employees, and thus will not lead to culture change. So, before engaging in culture change, make sure that there are compelling strategic and performance reasons to do so.

But even if there are compelling strategic reasons to change your organizational culture, you still may not want to engage in this work. Perhaps you would be uncomfortable with the personal authenticity culture change requires. Perhaps you don't want to engage in the difficult conversations that are almost always created by culture change. Perhaps you don't think you have the skills needed to manage this kind of change.

Of course, managing culture change is not for everyone. And there are many jobs for business leaders that do not require culture change. However, if there are compelling strategic reasons why you should engage in culture change, but you avoid doing so because you are not comfortable with this kind of change process, then the results presented in this book will be particularly valuable to you.

You see, in the end, the "secret" of culture change that we describe in this book is that there is no "secret" to culture change. Building culture-changing stories is a skill, something you can learn, a set of techniques you can refine. Your first culture-changing stories may not be as profound as some of the stories we will share with you in this book, but that does not mean they will have no impact on your organization's culture. And as you become more practiced at building culture-changing stories, those stories will become more profound and more impactful.

In the end, this book describes a set of skills you can learn and implement to build culture-changing stories. The book can teach you these skills, but it cannot give you the will to engage in culture change. That is entirely yours. That is why culture change must always begin with introspection to understand whether or not the changes you are contemplating are authentic to you and your personal values, and thus whether or not you have the will to engage in culture change. These issues are taken up in the next chapter.

CHAPTER THREE

Building Authentic Stories

Culture change begins by building authentic stories. Your stories are authentic when they reflect your deeply held values and beliefs about who you are as a leader, your commitment to the well-being of your employees and other stakeholders, and how these are related to the ability of your firm to implement your strategies. In this sense, authentic stories reveal to your employees something fundamental about who you are and what you want to accomplish.

For this reason, authentic stories reassure your employees that your commitment to cultural change is real and unchangeable. They know that your efforts to change the culture are not a whim, or ego-driven, or a transitory commitment, but instead are a manifestation of who you are as a person. When they hear the authentic stories you have built, they are more likely to join with you to cocreate your organization's new culture.

But when the stories you build are inauthentic, they can have exactly the opposite effect. Your employees can smell hypocrisy miles away. And if the stories you build do not reflect who you are as a person, they will be dismissed by your employees as manipulative and dishonest. These employees will not work with you to cocreate your organization's new culture.

Building Your Own Authentic Stories

Building authentic stories can be risky. Such stories may reveal more about who you are to your employees than you necessarily would prefer. Moreover, despite their authenticity, the stories you build may nevertheless be rejected by your employees as hollow and vacuous. The stories you build may show your employees the gap between where you want to be and where you are—we are all short of living our highest values. The stories you build may be dismissed as dishonest and manipulative.

Ultimately, building authentic stories plants a stake in the culture-change ground and reassures your employees of your commitment to this process. With such assurance, employees can join with you to cocreate your new culture.

Consider how building authentic stories affected the ability of several different business leaders to change their organizational cultures.

Authentic Story Building Begins with Insight

First, consider the experience of a young plant manager in a global corporation who questioned his own leadership capabilities in a way that led him to alter his entire approach to leadership.

> **STORY 3.1 "What If This Plane Crashed?"**
> **The chief manufacturing officer of a giant global corporation**
>
> I had been put in charge of a large plant in South America. For several years, this business had not been making money. The problem was so chronic that the CEO of the company visited us and said that if we couldn't fix the problem, they were going to consider exiting the business.
>
> I was just the manager of one of the plants in this segment, but they put me in charge of the team to solve this problem. They gave us 18 months to develop a plan to break even. I had responsibility for everything we would need—finance, marketing, product supply—to break even. And every three to four months, the CEO would meet with us to review progress.
>
> To get to one of these meetings, we took a company plane. This was my first trip on a corporate jet. I was the least senior person on the plane. I also didn't know a lot of the people from corporate. So, I took a seat in the back of the plane next to a window and sat quietly. I thought to myself, "This is going to be a great opportunity to get my presentation down to a couple of pages that lays out a really workable scenario." That was my hope.
>
> In fact, folks began talking among themselves. But they were not engaging with me, even though I was the one who was going to put the plan before the CEO. Instead, the conversation got "fluffier and fluffier," with no appreciation of what would actually need to be done to turn the business around.
>
> After more than one hour listening to them, I became pretty frustrated with this group of people. It was becoming clear that their conversation

would not help me or the review we were about to go through. At one point, I remember looking out the window, down at the huge forest we were flying over, and an interesting thought crossed my mind: "If this plane crashed, I don't know exactly what I would do to get out of the jungle. But the one thing I do know for sure is that I would not follow any of these people."

And then another thought struck me: "What if I was in a plane with my people, and the plane crashed? Would the people who work for me follow me?"

I remembered hearing a speech once at West Point. The title of the presentation was something like "Leading When the Lives of Others Depend on Your Decisions." The first point was that in these settings, you don't have time to develop detailed lists of issues, lots of presentations, brainstorming, and so on. Decisions need to be made, they need to be made quickly, and they need to be followed automatically.

For this to happen, leaders must demonstrate three things to subordinates before these kinds of decisions are made: First, that they are competent—that is, that they have the skills needed to make correct decisions and get the job done. Second, that they have character—that they are trustworthy and will put the interests of the team ahead of their own personal interests. And third, that they care about their team members as people.

Since that day on the corporate jet, I have tried to exemplify these three attributes of a leader in all my decisions and actions.

This business leader had to be honest with himself. Sure, he was annoyed at the other managers on the plane, how they were either unable or unwilling to engage the real challenges he was facing. But in a moment of clear personal insight, he also wondered whether or not his own people would be willing to rely on him, to trust his competence, his character, and his caring.

This moment of insight ended up informing the rest of this leader's career.

Revealing My Inexperience to My Employees

You don't have to be a plant manager to have these kinds of insights, nor do you have to accumulate years of experience to have them. Consider the case of Michael Schutzler, who learned about his approach to leadership—and used it to build a story that helped a project team succeed—when he was a very young manager.

STORY 3.2 "I Was Just a Young Kid and Needed to Change
the Conversation"
Michael Schutzler as project manager at Harris Corporation

I graduated from Penn State University with a degree in engineering. I was
quick, and was in the right place at the right time—I helped get a major
contract over the finish line for my first employer—and so they said, "He's
not just an engineer, he has leadership potential." So I became a management trainee.

After a short period of time, I was assigned my first project. Here I am,
I'm 23 years old, I was good at math and spreadsheets, but I'd never managed anyone or anything in my life. And I walk into the first meeting of the
project team, and there are a dozen or so people there—and the youngest
one is 40 years old. Of course, everyone in that room is leaning back in their
chairs, looking at me, and thinking, "Uh-huh. Yeah, right. Whatever."

So I started the meeting with a great deal of excitement and enthusiasm about this project we were going to work on together. But as I was talking, I was also reading the room. The body language I saw was stiff and
not very enthusiastic. A few people were shaking their heads—either in disagreement or disbelief, I couldn't tell.

This was the most transformative moment in my career. In that moment,
I had enough self-awareness to realize, "Michael, you have no credibility
with these people and you're telling them what to do. Why don't you just
stop, and ask them what to do?"

And so, I stopped talking.

I took a deep breath, and said, "Let me start over. I'm sorry. I've been
put in charge of this project, and I've never managed a project before. And
all of you have a lot more experience than me. I want the project to be successful, and I'm sure you want to be part of a successful project too. I want
to learn from you. You tell me what you need me to do in order for this
project to be successful, so that you're successful, and my commitment to
you is I will go do it."

This completely changed the dynamic of the conversation, and now lots
of ideas came out. I learned in that first hour everything I need to know
about project management because they all told me what do to, and I went
and did what I had committed I would do. I got the resources, the permis-
sions, and the approvals. I got all the things they wanted.

At the next team meeting, I said, "Okay, I did all the things you guys asked me to do. What's next?" And so we created a project together that was super successful for the company. I got a series of promotions as a result.

What I learned in that moment when the team was ignoring me was that if a team is going to be successful as a team, then the team has to lead. You've got to give the people in the room the power to decide where we're going to go. In this setting, my job is just to make sure that the direction the team decides to go makes sense. And I've been leading like that ever since.

I don't lead from the front. I lead from behind. I encourage other people to take risks. I encourage them to learn, to grow, and I make suggestions along the way. I've been doing this for so long now that—sure, I know a lot, and I can make recommendations right at the beginning of a project. But even now, I kind of shut up at the beginning of a project, and say, "What do you think we should do? Where should we go? What's possible?"

Of course, it took courage for Michael to step into a project management role, especially with so many more experienced managers reporting to him. But in many ways it took even more courage to recognize his lack of experience and his need to call on his more experienced colleagues for their help. Courage and humility. Building this story in the first meeting of his team not only changed the culture in this project team, but ultimately led Michael to develop an approach to leadership and management that informed his entire career.

Will My Authentic Stories Be Rejected by My Employees?

Because authentic stories are so intimate, the business leaders we interviewed knew that building them in their organizations would make them personally vulnerable. They knew that some people in their firm would love them for their honesty, while others would hate them for their temerity in challenging the status quo. They knew that some would see them as an organizational hero taking personal risks trying to rescue the firm from its own cultural dead ends, while others would see them as self-serving and conniving villains trying to make an imprint on the firm solely to gratify their pride and assuage their inexhaustible ego. Building authentic stories implies that a leader puts his or her most deeply held beliefs "out there" for public comment and scrutiny.

Of course, the mythology in the public press and in many organizations is that business leaders are protected by their organizational power, and thus invulnerable to the emotional vicissitudes that may be created by revealing their most personal selves through the stories they build. In this myth, how people in an organization judge a leader's values and beliefs is irrelevant—so what if they conclude that the leader is a villain they come to loathe? All that matters is that these people do what the leader tells them to do. As the saying goes, if a business leader wants a friend, she should get a dog.

The reality among the business leaders we interviewed was more nuanced. On the one hand, they understood that their position in the organization gave them some protection from the judgment of others about their personal values and beliefs. For some, this protection made it easier for them to be open and authentic, and thus easier for them to build effective culture-changing stories. Indeed, one could argue that for these reasons, business leaders are uniquely well positioned to actually create culture change in an organization.

On the other hand, these leaders also knew that they were not fully separate from the challenges that cultural change would create in their firm. They knew that such changes would be gut-wrenching for at least some of their employees and stakeholders. They knew that some employees would react very negatively to these changes and judge them and their motivations very harshly. They were not happy about being judged in this way—it wasn't something they looked forward to or relished—but accepted it as a necessary part of the culture-change process.

Consider the experience of Stefano Rettore, as he tried to build a new culture in a well-established business in the agriculture sector.

Story 3.3 "This Is Why I Am Who I Am"
Stefano Rettore as president of origination and member of the executive council at Archer Daniels Midland Corporation

Just a few months after I joined ADM, I was asked to lead the global agriculture business. I was new to the company. I was not part of the ADM culture. I was not even an American, and they asked me to lead the largest division in what was a very American company. I felt I faced a steep learning curve and needed to build a relationship with my management team.

But I didn't know who these people were—I knew their names and I knew their job histories, but I really didn't know them more deeply, and they didn't know me. For example, I didn't know their family stories, I didn't know who they were as people. But I didn't have a lot of time. I was new, we had to start operating at a higher level, and there was tremendous pressure to deliver results.

I decided to go off with my team for two days to discuss our operating plan and how to improve it. That was all very basic and normal, but I was convinced that wasn't going to be enough to build the kind of team spirit that we needed. So I decided that we would start the meeting differently.

In our first session together, I started with the following observation: "Look. I'm going to do something that I don't know if it's going to work out, but I feel it's the right thing to do. You don't know me, I don't know you that well, and we are going to work together. I believe that psychological safety is fundamental in team dynamics, and this is going to be important because we will make mistakes as we try to improve our performance. If we trust each other, then we will be able to admit to and fix these mistakes. But if we don't trust each other, we will continue to make these mistakes, and our performance will not improve. So, to begin to learn about each other, I'd like us all to share a story about how we became who we are as people and as leaders."

I knew I would have to start, so I thought a great deal about what story to tell about myself. It couldn't be something silly. It had to speak to some fundamental aspects of who I was as a person and how I came to be in this position. So I started by talking about my personal ambition and drive and where they came from.

"I lost my father when I was 19. He was diagnosed on December 15 and died 20 days later on January 5. That experience helped me realize how fast things can change in life—I went from having a father to not having a father in just a couple of weeks. I came to accept losing a father as just a part of life. And then, 10 years later, my little sister passed away. She was nine months pregnant, and her unborn son did not survive. And once again, my life changed overnight. These experiences have shaped me to believe that time is precious. We don't know when we are going to run out of time. So these experiences have made me into what I am today. I don't want to waste time doing things I don't believe in. I don't want to waste time in silly politics. I want to be transparent. I want to enjoy the people I'm with. I want to work hard but also enjoy life. I hope everybody around me wants the same thing. And yes, I am focused on growth more than cost cutting, because I think we have the opportunity to do something different, and life is short. And that's why I believe and act the way I do."

I didn't know how this story would influence others on the team. But members of the team began to share their stories. They told things about themselves that even colleagues of over 20 years did not know. They explained where their managerial values and goals came from. And all this occurred in an environment where we did not really know each other. It was very emotional, very real. Very vulnerable.

I think this meeting put in motion a very positive dynamic in the team. Of course, we talked about our operating plan and how to improve it, but we did so in a context of openness and trust. When I left the job, one and a half years after that meeting, several colleagues called me and said, "This has been the best 18 months I've had in the company." Some of these leaders had decades of experience. It was the best recognition I could have in one of the largest companies in the world. One senior executive called me to say that I had brought transparency and a more human approach to the company and that had made a huge difference. And it showed up in the bottom line, where we grew faster and were materially more profitable.

I believe it all started at that first meeting. I didn't say that anything I said in that meeting had to be kept confidential. In fact, I imagine that my personal story was told and retold throughout the organization. It was important to share the experiences that made me who I am. I continued to try to do that in many other ways, but taking the risk in the first meeting of doing something that could go very wrong was critical. But, like I said to the team, "I'd rather be wrong being who I am than be right by doing what's safe to do. I would rather build on a foundation of who I really am. If I fail, I will have failed doing what I believed in." It was a difficult choice, but it worked out really well.

By starting the first meeting of his team with a very personal story, Stefano was building a story that would fundamentally affect the culture of this part of ADM. Sharing that story took a leap of faith. He didn't know for sure how his employees would respond. When they responded by sharing their own stories, Stefano was well along the path of creating a new culture.

We All Fall Short of Living Our Own Values

Creating a new organizational culture is always aspirational. It's aspirational for your organization since you are asking members of your organization to put aside the familiar for the unfamiliar. But it is also aspirational for you, because maybe you don't fully understand all the values and beliefs that will be part of this new culture. And maybe, even if you do understand these values, you don't always live up to them.

If culture change required that you fully understood and perfectly lived the values of the new culture you are trying to create, then culture change would never occur. All business leaders, at all levels of an organization, sooner or later fall short in understanding what the new culture they are trying to build is, and fall short in living the values of this culture even when they understand them.

Because of these personal limitations, stories that you build that pretend you fully understand and live the values of a new culture are—by definition—inauthentic. Your people won't believe these stories. They will dismiss them as manipulative and dishonest.

However, these weaknesses do not disqualify you from leading cultural change. Indeed, how you respond to your personal shortcomings can help you build a story that can actually facilitate cultural change. Your failings can be used to demonstrate your authenticity because they increase your vulnerability. This sounds counterintuitive, but consider the example of Carl Thong, a serial entrepreneur and currently group managing director at Momenta, a leadership training company headquartered in Singapore.

> **STORY 3.4 "I Am Not All I Want to Be"**
> **Carl Thong as group managing director at Momenta**
>
> Two things that are central in my leadership style are honoring what I say and being honorable. But I sometimes fall short.
>
> Six months ago, one of my leaders came to me with a document that summarized the work that he had been doing. I was walking out of the office door after a long day when he gave me the paper. I was really tired. But I looked at the document and immediately pointed out 10 mistakes. I said to my employee, "John, you've got to stop giving me this bullshit!" and gave him back the document before I walked out to my car. I drove home and,

in the car, immediately knew that I had not handled that situation well. It was on my mind.

When I got home, I had dinner with my family. Then I got a text message from John. He said, "Dear Carl, I would like to let you know what the dictionary definition of the word bullshit is. It means 'written nonsense.' I don't feel that I gave you bullshit. I tried my best. If it's not good, you can tell me, but why did you use this word 'bullshit' with me? I just want to let you know that I don't really feel good about it, and I apologize for making you upset, but I felt it's important to share this thought with you."

I saw his message, and it was an aha moment for me. I wasn't living up to my own standards. I was not behaving honorably. I immediately texted him back and said, "John, thank you for correcting me. Thank you for calling me out. I am not living the values that we set for everyone in the company. This is an amazing reminder that I have a lot to improve on myself."

He texted back, "Oh, good. I was praying the whole time that you weren't going to be angry." I replied, "No, I'm not angry and I'm very appreciative of you pointing this problem out. Can you do me a favor? Can you share this encounter with me with the whole company?"

So, this story has become an example of one of our key values—honoring what we say and being honorable. This is one of our cultural benchmarks even though we often fail to live up to this standard. But if we acknowledge when we fall short and then recommit to try our best to get back to these standards, then it's okay. That story has been retold many times by my staff and by other employees throughout the company and has become important for creating a culture of honor in our company.

Some CEOs think that if they ever slip up on the cultural values they are trying to create in a firm, their hypocrisy will be found out and their efforts will come to naught. Some have concluded that, given this threat, it is better to not try to change a culture at all than it is to try and fail.

But these kinds of missteps are inevitable. The point is not to pretend that they will not emerge, the point is to minimize them—of course—but when they occur, to use them as an opportunity to reinforce the cultural change you are trying to create. Your mistakes can become stories that give everyone permission to try and fail, but then to try again to live a new set of values.

Planting a Stake in the Ground

In the end, one of the most important things that building authentic stories does is make it clear to your employees just how committed you are to culture change. Your commitment can create employee commitment which, in turn, can lead to the cocreation of a new culture.

Consider the example of the authenticity of Dan Burton, CEO of a rapidly growing firm in the health care sector.

> **STORY 3.5** **"If We Want Our Team Members to Embrace Humility, I Must Be Humble; If We Want Our Team Members to Embrace Transparency, I Must Be Transparent"**
> **Dan Burton as CEO at Health Catalyst**
>
> Two of the critical aspects of the culture at Health Catalyst are humility and transparency. But it's very hard to scale these kinds of values—especially as you are growing rapidly. We went from just a few team members to more than 1,500 team members and contractors in just over 10 years.
>
> These values have to begin with me. So, for example, each year I have an anonymous 360-degree review. From the beginning, I decided to share my results with the entire company. I think vulnerability is an incredibly important part of servant leadership. It helps debunk the notion that leaders are perfect or even need to be perfect. None of us is. I think it's incredibly empowering for team members to see that leaders recognize—with humility—that there will always be opportunities for improvement. So I share my 360-degree results on an annual basis.
>
> Also, in our company-wide team meetings every two to four weeks we have an "Ask Leadership Anything" part of the agenda. We average about 30 to 40 questions that get submitted, in real time, to the company leadership, in addition to the 10 to 20 questions that are submitted in advance. These questions can be anonymous or can include the submitter's name. I am in the meeting, of course, along with three or four other members of the senior leadership team. One of us answers, or tries to answer, every one of these questions. And if we don't know the answer, we will the next time we get together in a couple of weeks.
>
> I view all these actions on my part as opportunities to demonstrate humility and transparency. This is especially true when the feedback is hard.

For example, we recently had to cut back on a benefit due to Covid. There were a few team members who submitted scathing responses to this change, some with very personal elements aimed directly toward me. I addressed all these responses in a company-wide team meeting.

Sometimes I need to apologize to my team, to acknowledge that I made a mistake. For example, one team member expressed frustration with our commitment to diversity and inclusion—that maybe we were paying too much attention to these issues. In my written response, I explained why we had this commitment but acknowledged that maybe sometimes the manner in which we approached this could have been more effective. I asked our team to be patient, because we were still learning in this area.

However, another team member read my response and reached out to me. She wrote that I should not have apologized for our efforts in these areas. I read her comments carefully and became persuaded that she was right. So I edited my initial response and then contacted her and thanked her for sharing her insights and ideas with me.

I don't have all the answers, and I don't always get things right the first time. Or the second time. And I have to be okay with everyone knowing that.

By living the values of humility and transparency, Dan Burton builds stories that make it difficult for him to back off his commitment to these values. And he builds these stories not just annually—when he shares his 360-degree evaluations—but every two weeks in his all-company team meetings.

Not surprisingly, the stories that Dan Burton builds have helped create a remarkable culture—one that is consistently evaluated as having among the most engaged employees in the country. He argues that this culture has been instrumental in helping his company grow from annual sales of less than $1 million 10 years ago to a market capitalization greater than $2 billion 10 years later.

What If You Don't Have Values Consistent with the New Culture?

As these stories demonstrate, culture change necessarily involves a business leader building authentic stories. But what if the values and beliefs held by a business leader are inconsistent with the culture change required to implement a firm's strategies? Building authentic stories in this setting will not enable culture change, it will make culture change less likely. If your core values and beliefs are inconsistent with the culture that you need to create in order to implement your strategies, what should you do?

In these settings, you really only have two choices. First, you can begin to undertake the personal transformation required to change your values, beliefs, and expectations about how your firm should operate. This can take time and effort, but you need to begin this process before you start to change your culture. Indeed, if you are honest with your employees that you are in the process of changing your personal values, they will often give you the benefit of the doubt. When you make mistakes and return to type, step up, admit your error and—as has already been suggested—your mistake can actually build a story to help implement your culture change.

Second, you can step aside. We know this sounds like a difficult choice. But if your core values are really inconsistent with the culture that needs to be created in order to implement your new strategy, staying on as a business leader will likely be a deeply dissatisfying experience. Consider how Steve Young, former NFL quarterback currently working in the private equity industry, worked with the former CEO of one of the firms his company had recently purchased.[1]

Story 3.6 "He Threw a Chair at Me!"
Steve Young as chairman and cofounder at Huntsman Gay Global Capital

Let me tell you about an experience I had with a business owner I'll call Michael. My private equity firm had bought the business from him, and we had some very difficult conversations around control. Essentially, my view was that only one person could be in control. If there wasn't one quarterback, things would devolve—and the quarterback needed to be the new CEO we hired. After we bought the business, Michael agreed to be the board chair and wouldn't be involved in day-to-day operations any longer. But Michael kept hanging around the business. Finally, the CEO called me and said, "Hey, this guy is driving me crazy." I had to call Michael and ask him to back off and give the new management some breathing room.

Michael answered, "Well, what do you want me to do? I can't even walk around the company?"

I said, "Look, in the end, it's about people giving people space."

Michael responded, "Okay, okay." However, about a month later, the CEO called me and said, "Look, it's either him or me!"

I called Michael and said, "We've got to meet. Let's get together." We met in the boardroom without the CEO. I started with a strong statement, "Michael, you've got to go." And that created an argument. This argument escalated to the point that Michael picked up a chair and threw it at me. He wasn't necessarily aiming for me, and he didn't mean to hurt me, but he threw the chair in frustration and anger.

All it was, in the end, was an inability to see each other's point of view. I knew that throwing a chair wasn't where I wanted the conversation to end. Our argument could have stopped the conversation at a standoff. Or I could have chosen to escalate it further. But I wanted to find common ground. Once it got dramatic, I realized it was time to slow down and get to the root of the problem.

When the chair went flying, I was initially startled. But then my reaction was almost cheery: "Really? Is that all you've got?" Michael took a deep breath and cracked the slightest grin. We looked at each other, then I said, "Okay, what are we going to do? Let's try to figure out what is driving this."

As we continued our conversation, I listened, and Michael talked. Eventually, he said, "Having this back-and-forth discussion with you, I just now realize that I either need to run the business, or I need to leave the business. It's how I am. It's who I am. I can't be the chair. I have to be in the business all the way, or I have to be out of it."

In the end, Michael realized that being out of the business altogether was really the best place for him as well as for the business. Even now, 10 years later, Michael and I stay in close contact. He calls me from the four corners of the earth, sending pictures of him holding his baby grand-daughter. He often says, "Steve, letting go of the business was the best thing that ever happened to me. I'm so grateful."

There is, of course, much to learn from this story. But from the point of view of the culture change that Steve's private equity firm was implementing in the company they had purchased, the essential truth was that if Michael had stayed on with the firm, not only would he have destroyed the company, he himself would have been much worse off. Who Michael was, as an individual, was simply inconsistent with what the firm had to become under its new ownership. In this setting, the decision to leave was not a manifestation of Michael's weakness but of his great strength, even courage.

Conclusion

Authenticity has been important in building and changing organizational cultures throughout history. Consider, for example, the task of building a cooperative culture within the Supreme Headquarters Allied Expeditionary Force (SHAEF)—the group assigned the task of planning and executing the invasion of Western Europe during the Second World War.

Rarely has a more heterogeneous group, with more conflicting personal and political interests, ever been assembled to execute such a historically important mission. SHAEF consisted of 14 military leaders from four countries (the United States, Great Britain, France, and the Soviet Union), representing army, air force, and naval operations. In addition, it was supported by seven staff members (for supplies, intelligence, and so forth) and five political officers from the United Kingdom and the United States.

This team, led by the Supreme Allied Commander General Dwight D. Eisenhower of the United States, ultimately commanded 2 million soldiers, sailors, and airmen from eight Allied countries, most of whom were crowded into camps in the United Kingdom.[2] Known as Operation Overlord, this would be the largest land, sea, and air operation ever attempted in the history of warfare.

However, SHAEF members disagreed on almost everything about the invasion of Europe: when it should happen (the Soviet Union had, for several years, lobbied for an early invasion to relieve pressure from the Nazi invasion of Russia, while the United States and United Kingdom were in favor of postponing the invasion until Allied troops were fully prepared), where it should happen (some members thought it should take place at the Pas-de-Calais in France, others at Normandy), who should be in command on the ground during the attack (this responsibility was ultimately given to British Field Marshal Montgomery), and the short-term and long-term objectives of the invasion (US leaders emphasized the importance of securing the port of Cherbourg, just west of the Normandy invasion site; British leaders focused on eliminating launch sites in northern France that the Nazis used for missile attacks on the United Kingdom; and French leaders emphasized the importance of recapturing Paris from the Nazis as soon as possible). In making these decisions, Eisenhower had to keep the interests of presidents and prime ministers and generals and field marshals in balance. His international coalition was rife with conflict, disagreement, and outsized egos—and yet needed to coalesce around a specific strategy for invading Europe. In short, Eisenhower had to build a cooperative culture in a setting where cooperation seemed virtually impossible.

Eisenhower turned out to be a perfect choice for this job. Born in Denison, Texas, and raised in Abilene, Kansas, the third of seven sons, Eisenhower came from a modest family background. He sought and obtained an appointment to the US Military Academy at West Point, not in search of a glorious military career, but because he didn't have the money for tuition at a nonmilitary school. After only a moderately successful prewar career, Eisenhower rose quickly in the ranks during the war, noted primarily for his ability to build consensus among conflicting interests in pursuing a single objective—winning the war.

Throughout his life, Eisenhower had two central values in his approach to leadership. First, he defined leadership as "the art of getting someone else to do something you want done because they want to do it." Eisenhower was known for his ability to listen intently and sincerely, and then to find ways to transcend conflicts among his staff. It was not uncommon for those who reported to Eisenhower to believe that they were the ones that had come up with some critical idea or suggestion to move Overlord along. From Eisenhower's point of view, it was amazing how much can get done when you don't care who gets credit.

Second, Eisenhower's approach was always understated, never confrontational. This was reflected in a plaque on his desk in the Oval Office, after he became the 34th president of the United States: "Suaviter in modo, fortiter in re" ("Gently in manner, strongly in deed"). He saw his peers berating their subordinates and characterized this as "assault, not leadership."

Not caring about who got the credit, and pursuing his objectives in a gentle understated way, created the possibility of cooperation within the SHAEF, even as centrifugal forces threatened to blow the alliance apart. Then, and throughout his career, Eisenhower's actions were fully authentic with respect to his two core leadership values. This was the case even when his reluctance to take credit may have, in some people's eyes, reduced his career opportunities.

One particularly telling example of how Eisenhower used his authentic commitment to these two leadership principles in implementing his preferred strategy had to do with the use of air power during the initial phases of the European invasion.[3] Eisenhower thought that the best way to ensure the success of the invasion (and to reduce casualties) was to use the Allied air forces to bomb transportation hubs in France and Germany in the weeks and days before the invasion. Eisenhower's theory was that the implementation of this "transportation strategy" would prevent the Nazis from concentrating their troops to repel the invasion. To implement this strategy, Eisenhower wanted to put the Allied air force under his direct command.

Allied air force commanders from both the United States and the United Kingdom rejected Eisenhower's "transportation strategy" and argued, instead, that bombing German manufacturing facilities would destroy Germany's ability to engage in war and would draw fighter planes away from the Normandy coast—both of which, in their view, would help support the invasion more effectively than bombing transportation hubs. Not surprisingly, these commanders also strongly resisted the request to put their air forces under Eisenhower's direct control.

Discussion about which of these strategies was superior is not the point of this example. The point is how Eisenhower went about resolving this conflict and how this process built a story about how decision making would unfold within the SHAEF. This process—which took over four months—involved Eisenhower and his team consulting with every major stakeholder in this decision and forcing these stakeholders to debate the issues until a consensus could be created. Then, when the time came, Eisenhower was able to implement his transportation strategy.

First, Eisenhower built a team of well-respected individuals from different countries and different military services who agreed with his strategic analysis. Then he began a series of meetings with the Combined Chiefs of Staff (the US and UK organizations to which the SHAEF reported), Winston Churchill, Franklin Roosevelt, and his team to discuss the importance of the transportation strategy.

At the same time, he and his team began discussions with the US and British air force commanders—the people who were most opposed to the implementation of the transportation strategy. Initial discussions with these "air barons" did not resolve the conflict. Indeed, in response to these meetings, they developed new plans to use their bombers to destroy Germany's oil production instead of supporting Eisenhower's transportation strategy.

But Eisenhower and his team continued their discussions with key stakeholders. Churchill and his war cabinet raised issues about the number of French civilian casualties the transportation strategy would create. And yet, Eisenhower and his team continued in these stakeholder discussions.

In January 1944, Eisenhower returned to the United States for consultations and rest. During his visit, he met several times with the US Army chief of staff, George Marshall, emphasizing the importance of the transportation strategy and the need to unify the command of the air force. Meanwhile, back in England, the "air barons" and British politicians were working to subvert Eisenhower's efforts. Upon returning to the United Kingdom, Eisenhower and his team were successful at resolving many logistical and strategic problems of Operation Overlord, but there was still no agreement on the transportation strategy.

In long meetings between Eisenhower, Churchill, and their respective staffs, a compromise—in principle—was finally hammered out. However, details of the implementation of this compromise continued to cause problems—Eisenhower wanted to command the Allied air forces, the commanders of the air forces only wanted Eisenhower to supervise their work. In the end, it was agreed that Eisenhower would "direct" the Allied air force.[4]

At some point in these last discussions, the long-suffering Eisenhower threatened to resign: "By God, you tell that bunch that if they can't get together and stop quarreling like children, I will quit. I will tell the Prime Minister to get someone else to run this damn war! I'll quit."[5] Note, however, that even in threatening to resign, Eisenhower did not tell his subordinates how to resolve their conflict, only that they must resolve this conflict.

In the end, Eisenhower was able to implement his transportation strategy with a largely unified command.

Perhaps the ultimate example of Eisenhower's authenticity to his core leadership values can be found in two speeches he wrote just before the Normandy invasion in June 1944.[6] The first was read to the soldiers, sailors, and airmen of the Allied Expeditionary Force the evening before the attack was to begin. It read, in part:

You are about to embark upon the Great Crusade, toward which we have striven these many months. The eyes of the world are upon you. The hopes and prayers of liberty-loving people everywhere march with you. . . . Your task will not be an easy one. Your enemy is well trained, well equipped, and battle hardened. He will fight savagely. But . . . I have full confidence in your courage, devotion to duty, and skill in battle. We will accept nothing less than full victory. Good luck. And let us all beseech the blessing of Almighty God upon this great and noble undertaking.

Eisenhower never gave the second speech. Handwritten on a scrap of paper, it was the speech he was going to give if the landings had not been successful.

Our landings in the Cherbourg-Havre area have failed to gain a satisfactory foothold and I have withdrawn the troops. My decision to attack at this time and place was based upon the best information available. The troops, the air and the navy did all that bravery and devotion to duty could do. If any blame or fault attaches to the attempt it is mine alone.

True to his core values, in the first speech, Eisenhower anticipates full victory and ascribes it entirely to the "courage, devotion, and skill" of his troops. In the second speech, authentic to the end, he acknowledges failure and takes the entire "blame or fault" on himself.

In your effort to change your culture, are you willing to be fully authentic to your core values and beliefs?

CHAPTER FOUR

Star in Your Own Story

You have probably already noticed something that all the stories we have shared so far have in common: they all involve business leaders doing something that had the effect of building a culture-changing story. For a story to have the potential to change an organization's culture, it must "star" the business leader.

The reasons for this are fairly obvious. Recall from Chapter 2 that one of the reasons why culture change is difficult is that employees often have good reason to question their leader's commitment to this change, especially when other business challenges begin to emerge. For many of these employees, even apparently sincere statements about the importance of culture and culture change are just not credible. They have seen how this kind of "cheap talk" has faltered in the past, leading to abandoned commitments, disappointed expectations, and a return to a historically dominant culture.

In this setting, it's not surprising that many employees—even those who see the value in changing an organization's culture—will limit their involvement in and commitment to cultural change. The smart play is to lay low—play the game, go to the training, sign the commitments, whatever. Suppose your firm is one of the handful that are actually able to change their culture. These cautious employees aren't much worse off for their caution about culture change. If, on the other hand, culture change really happens, great. They double down on their commitments and become part of the change once it actually occurs.

But what if an effort to change an organization's culture doesn't take? Indeed, the data suggests that this is the rational expectation for most culture-change projects. Employees who have gone all in on a culture change can find themselves in a very uncomfortable situation—being a leading supporter of a culture change that has failed. As a result of this failure, they may be asked to leave. Or, if not asked, they may choose to leave on their own to find a place where their preferred culture already exists.

The Culture-Change Death Spiral

In this sense, deciding whether or not to support a culture change can often be about deciding whether or not to change jobs. Naturally, many employees—especially in the face of such high failure rates for culture-change efforts—will be cautious about making these commitments.

Ironically, this caution can be one of the reasons why a culture-change effort fails. This, then, becomes the self-fulfilling prophecy presented in Figure 4.1—lack of employee commitment to changing an organization's culture can reduce the likelihood of such a change taking place, which in turn reduces the willingness of employees to commit to enabling such a change, which reduces the likely success of such a change effort, and so forth.

You can play a vital role in stopping the emergence of this "death spiral." This happens when you credibly signal your irreversible commitment to culture change. However, simple verbal assertions that you are "really, really committed to culture change" are not enough. They are still just "cheap talk."

Stopping the Death Spiral

Instead, you must put your money where your mouth is. One way to do this is to link, in a very direct (and costly to reverse) way, a story you build to

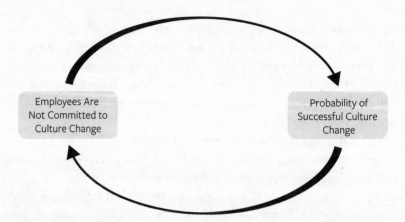

FIGURE 4.1.   Employee Commitment to Culture Change and the Probability That Culture-Change Efforts Will Be Successful

support culture change with yourself as an individual. In short, you must star in your own culture-changing story. Thus, these stories

- Can't be just about some inspirational figure in history ("These are the leadership principles I learned from Abraham Lincoln.")
- Can't just be funny stories from which important management lessons can be learned ("Three CEOs walk into a bar . . .")
- Can't be inspirational stories about another employee in the firm ("Let me tell you about the customer service exemplified by Jane Doe in the Atlanta store.")
- Can't be just strongly worded statements about your commitment to culture change ("I'm really committed to culture change. Really.")
- Can't just be a list of your vision and values ("My core values are honesty, integrity, and commitment—just like every other business leader in the world.")

Instead, you have to do something that builds a culture-changing story.

"Build" in the phrase "build a story" is a transitive verb. If you are not willing to do something that will build a story in your firm to help change its culture, then it is very unlikely that your employees will believe that you are truly committed to culture change. And without that commitment— death spiral.

Consider the story built by Annette Friskopp, when she was a new employee in a small high-technology company—a story that had an impact on the culture of not only that company but many other companies where she worked over her career.

Star in Your Own Story

STORY 4.1 "I Need to Get on the Boats"
Annette Friskopp as executive vice president at a fleet management company—name kept confidential

My first job out of school was at a satellite fleet management company. We built and sold systems to track and monitor different kinds of ships and boats. When I joined the company, it was very new. There had been some investment, but things were not going that well. At one critical meeting,

I was sitting with the CEO and another person he had hired. He gave us the classic speech: "Look to your left, look to your right. I can't afford to keep paying both of you, so one of you is going to be gone in three weeks."

I immediately stood up and headed for the door. With my hand on the doorknob, the CEO asked, "Where are you going?" I said, "I'm wasting time sitting here talking to you guys. I know what we need to do. We need to go get customers, we need to sell, so I'm wasting my time sitting here." I walked down the hall to the travel department to book a flight. "Where do you want to go?" Good question. I didn't know for sure where I should go to meet customers, I just knew I needed to go. So I said, "I need to go to . . . New Orleans." I chose New Orleans because it was the only place I could think of where there were fleets of boats. I grew up on a farm in Nebraska, and when my daddy sold his grain, it went on a big truck down to a boat, down the Mississippi River to New Orleans, and was then put on big ships and sold all around the world. So I knew there were fleets of vessels there. Besides, my competition had been focusing on the West Coast, and this was pretty much open territory.

So, I'm flying out to New Orleans, and I'm literally getting so excited to look down on the Mississippi River, and I'm like, "There are boats! There are barges! There are fleets of vessels!" I get to some crappy Holiday Inn, and I throw my bags in my room, and I go, "Now what do I do?" The Yellow Pages! There was no Internet back then, so I get the battered, big New Orleans Yellow Pages, and I put it on that horrible bedspread, and I'm flipping through, and I go, "B: boats, boats, boats." In the Yellow Pages ads, it's all about fishing boats, pontoon boats, and "rent a fishing boat for the weekend."

I paused for a second. I shouldn't be looking under "boats." I should be looking under "barges." So I go to "barges" in the Yellow Pages, and I find listings for buying barges, cleaning barges, towing barges, and so forth. Then it hit me—my customers were probably the companies that towed barges on the Mississippi.

So I started calling towboat companies in New Orleans. I would get the operator and they would say, "Who would you like to speak with?" I was like, "Umm, who oversees your fleets? Your fleet manager?" They would say, "Oh, that is Mr. So-and-so. Just a minute and I'll put you through."

I got through to the fleet manager at about three companies. Here was my pitch: "I am from California, and we have some interesting technology for communications rather than your VHF radios. I want to understand how you use your VHF radios and how they are limited." I remember one of them saying, "Well, sure, young lady! Come on down! I'd love to speak with you!" That was my first appointment.

I get in this guy's office, and he is sitting in a nice, all-glass office building, and I say to myself, "I'm not going to learn much about how these towboats are operated sitting in a glass tower." So I basically interviewed him and said, "How do you run a fleet of boats? How do you communicate with them to know when they need supplies? How do you bill for their work?" I jokingly asked him, "Do you just sit up here in your office and watch them go by?" He asked, "Have you ever ridden on the river?" I said, "No." "Would you like to?" I said, "Sure." Within a day I was invited to ride the barges from Baton Rouge down to New Orleans to get closer to our prospective customers.

If you've never sat in the wheelhouse of a towboat on the Mississippi River, let me tell you, it's amazing. We were pushing half a mile of barges lashed to our boat with over 10,000-horsepower dual engines. Running downriver it takes two miles to stop one of those floating masses.

As I sat with the captain on that trip, I peppered him with questions: "What's the paperwork you fill out?" He showed me these big green ledgers with different instructions for filling out different forms—for barge drop-offs and barge pickups. I said, "Now, what do you do with all this information? When do you send it in to your office?" Pointing to one of the huge green sheets, maybe two feet tall and three feet wide, he said, "Well, when the sheet is full, I send it in to Houston." I asked, "How long does it take to fill up a sheet?" He said, "Maybe four weeks or so, when I have enough barge drops and pickups." I said, "How do you bill your customers?" He said, "Well, it's after this paper gets mailed into Houston."

After a couple of days in New Orleans, I drove over to Houston, to this company's headquarters, to follow where those big green sheets went. I visited floors of data entry operators keying the barge drop information into an old Unix system. Next, someone in the sales department compared the keyed data to the sales contract—to see if what was dropped was what was supposed to be dropped, and what was the price that was quoted for this service.

It could take up to 90 days between the time when there was a barge drop-off and when an invoice was generated to get paid for that service.

I went back to California and built a software system for fleet management—a tracking system for fleet logistics and electronic billing. And we built touch-screen onboard software so that captains could drag and drop barge icons onscreen to enter drops-offs and pickups into the system right there in their wheelhouse. From there it went by satellite to their headquarters and was automatically compared to the associated sales contract for pricing. Then an invoice was generated within 90 seconds and sent by electronic data interchange (EDI) to the customers. This software dramatically changed the cash flow for the barge industry.

I captured 90 percent of this market. Every towboat operator, every barge operator, had to have this software because in the old system so much of their cash flow was tied up waiting for collections. So, once one operator got this software, every operator needed to get this software.

I've shared this story many times in my career. I use it to set expectations about how we go into the field with customers to understand how they work and how we can improve their business. I want to drive curiosity. I want all employees to have that sense of curiosity to follow the paper trail. What do your customers do? What do they need to accomplish? How does their business run? And can we then improve it with our capabilities? That is the mindset I want to create.

When we went into the fisheries industry, I did a similar type of thing with the commercial fishing fleets off the East Coast of the United States. I spent time out on the boats, to see, for example, how scallop harvesting was being monitored. We replaced onboard observers—yes, people on the deck counting fish and bags—with a computerized Vessel Monitoring System that monitored the fisheries for the National Marine Fisheries Service and added the benefit of connecting all the boats in a firm's fleet, through satellites, to headquarters to improve communications and logistics. That way, the productivity of the fleet as a whole could be monitored so that the fleet could harvest as many scallops as they were allowed, per the government quota.

This is what I want my sales reps and engineers to do—not just sell what we have but be able to learn the needs and challenges of our customers, and then think about how we can use what we have or what we can create to solve our customers' problems. To do that, we need to understand our customers' problems—we have to go out into the field and experience what our customers are experiencing.

Initially, all Annette wanted to do was to keep her job. And she knew that meant she couldn't be hanging around corporate headquarters wondering about what her customers might need. She had to go out to the field, to be with her customers. And in boldly going where no one had gone before, Annette began creating a sales culture in her company, a sales culture that has served her well during her entire career.

Annette could have asked a sales associate to go out to the field—to go to New Orleans, Baton Rouge, Houston. But Annette was starring in her own story.

It is also appropriate to note that when Annette was doing all this going out, she was one of a very few women operating in the vessel fleet management business. But Annette never let other people's assumptions prevent her from doing what she knew needed to be done. Her personal courage in going out to the customers made the stories she was building about a sales culture even more powerful.

When it comes to culture change, your deeds are more important than your words. Don't get us wrong, your inspirational words can help explain and motivate the need for cultural change—something that is discussed in more detail in Chapter 8. But words without deeds are cheap and have limited impact. When you start "being the culture" you are trying to create, then culture change can begin.

Being the Star When Things Don't Go Well

It's not always easy to be the star of your culture-change story. This is especially the case when your efforts to change your organization's culture are not going well. Consider Michael Schutzler's experience in a startup:

> **STORY 4.2 "I Wrote the Values on the Wall"**
> **Michael Schutzler as founder and CEO at FreeShop**
>
> I was 35 years old, and I was building my first startup. I had read somewhere that if you wanted a startup to be successful, you needed to have a strong organizational culture, and that culture had to be based on some values. That didn't sound very difficult to me, so I wrote up a list of values. I wrote down five values and felt really good about them. I said to myself, "I've got this culture thing locked down; this list of values is what we are going to do in the company in terms of our culture." So, I had the five values printed on a wall so that every employee would see them when they walked through the front door.

But even in the early days of my career, I developed the habit of trying to get feedback, to see how things are going. So I asked a number of employees what they thought about my list of values—confident that they would see the wisdom in what I had done. Many of their responses surprised me, "You know, don't you, that list of values is a joke." I was shocked. And offended. Pointing to the list, I said, "No! I really mean this. These are the values I want to build the company's culture around."

Their replies continued to surprise me, "I'm sure you really do mean these things, Michael. They are your values. But they don't represent our company. We don't live up to these values. They are nothing like us. We should write up there what we are, not what you think we should be."

That last comment was like a BOOM! in my head—it really caught my attention. Of course, they were right. My list of values was just that—a list of my values. And so, we started having some discussions about what our real values were and what we wanted them to be. We erased my list from the wall and started to talk about "What are we?" and "What will make us successful?" and "What do we want to be to continue our success?"

It was those discussions that revealed the truth of where we actually were and what we thought we needed to do better in order to be successful next year and the year after.

This was an important lesson for me. For example, one of the values that I had put on my list was that we would have fun at work. Look, we all worked very hard—it was a startup. Everybody was working 100 hours a week and they were exhausted, so I wanted to make sure that we always remembered that we were doing this because we wanted to and we had to find a way of making this fun, even though it was hard work.

Turns out that having fun at work was not high on most of our employees' list of priorities. What they said is that they were in this thing to take our company public. They wanted to make a lot of money. Yes, they were entrepreneurs and they wanted to change the world. But they wanted to become wealthy in the process.

Besides that, they each had their own way of having fun. Some liked playing basketball, others cooking with a friend, and so forth. So, for many of our employees, having fun at work was not that important. They didn't want the company wasting their time trying to bring fun into their lives instead of focusing on going public.

What they did say was that winning—defined as taking the company public—was very important to them. They agreed that winning in that way could be fun. So, if winning was a core value of the company's culture, then they could buy into that—and when we won, that would be fun. But having fun itself was not a core value.

By recognizing his own mistake, Michael built a story that exemplified humility and an openness to learning. Suppose that someone besides Michael, the CEO, had crafted this list of values. Would that list have generated the same kind of impact that Michael's list created? Probably not. But it was Michael who posted that list, and Michael who discovered his mistake, and Michael who quickly fixed his mistake. And because Michael was starring in his own story, the impact of that story on the culture at this startup was substantial.

Taking Responsibility for a Product Failure

Michael's experience suggests that a business leader's mistakes can be an important source of culture-changing stories. Indeed, we have seen this in other stories as well, including Manoel Amorim's story (Story 1.1) where a service failure was used to build a story, and Carl Thong's story (Story 3.4) where a business leader's rash reaction to a subordinate was used to build a culture-changing story.

Another business leader we interviewed shared how taking responsibility for a product failure helped build a culture of accountability in his plant.

STORY 4.3 "Taking Responsibility for My Mistakes"
The chief manufacturing officer of a giant global corporation

I was a plant manager at one of the company sites in Latin America. That plant had a cleaning product—a local brand—that was very successful in the market. The idea came up to extend this product line with an extra product benefit. A small team concluded that this could be done relatively easily and fast. Everyone agreed, and we launched a reformulated product in the market.

Two weeks after the launch, our distributors were sending the new product back. If you opened a bottle, it smelled bad. Despite doing stability tests and validating the new formulation, the formula was wrong. It was clearly out of balance.

When the product started coming back, and it was obviously bad, we spent the first days trying to assign, and avoid, blame. Was it the commercial function or the technical function that had caused the problem? Was it the cost and the timing of the product or the robustness of the formula?

After some time with this finger-pointing mindset, I was in my office, looking at a bottle of this product. I turned it over and read, printed on the back label, that it had been made in this plant. My immediate thought was—who is the manager of this plant? It's me! So, who is responsible? It's me! It doesn't matter who was guilty, who made the mistake. The truth is, this was my plant, and I was responsible.

As soon as I realized this, I decided that I needed to take the lead on fixing the problem. So I picked up the phone and called our regional headquarters. I talked to the commercial and technical officers, saying, "We have a problem, the problem happened in my plant, and I am responsible. We need to retrieve the product from stores, we need to dispose of the bad product in an environmentally correct way, and we need to reformulate and then reintroduce the product. Our operations are very small and we don't have the resources to do these things. Can you help us? Can you send us the people we need?"

I went on, "After we sort this out and are back to producing a great product, we are going to understand the root causes of this problem. We're going to learn about the causes so this can never happen again. But I am not interested in who is guilty for making the mistake. And I already know who is responsible for it—that's me. So, we're going to get to work and fix the problem and make sure it never happens again."

Accepting the responsibility that comes with managing an organization is an essential feature of every successful operation I have ever been associated with. My most recent job was coordinating the supply chains for all the company's factories worldwide. If someone in the organization made the wrong forecast and we end up with too much inventory, it does not matter who made the forecast—you own the inventory, so this is your responsibility. If they made the wrong forecast, and you don't have all you need to serve your customers, it doesn't matter who made the forecast—you own capacity, so it's your responsibility.

By taking responsibility, we waste less time trying to figure out who is to blame for a mistake, and more time fixing the mistake and making sure it never happens again.

This business leader was making a clear statement about the kind of culture he wanted at his plant. He would no longer tolerate a culture of placing blame on someone else, and would only accept people taking responsibility for their own actions. He was building a culture-changing story.

However, the story became more credible because instead of just asking people to take responsibility for their actions, he took responsibility. By starring in his own story, this business leader built a story that had a profound impact on the culture of his plant.

And, by the way, the cleaning product with the extra product benefit became a best seller in its market.

You Are the Star, but Don't Go It Alone

To set the example of what a new culture can be, you must be that new culture. That inevitably means that you must star in the culture-changing stories you build. However, at the same time, you cannot be alone when building these stories. It helps if others are with you, to see your example, to understand its implications for the culture you are trying to create. You are the star, but you must have costars who can tell and retell the story you are building.

Alberto Carvalho, a leader of the Gillette division within Procter & Gamble, understood this as he tried to change the product development culture at this company.

STORY 4.4 "I'm Going to India"
Alberto Carvalho as vice president, Global Gillette Business at Procter & Gamble

When I first joined Gillette, I was made responsible for the emerging market business—all the countries in Africa, South America, Asia, and so forth. It didn't take long to figure out that we were actually not doing very well in those markets. We had countries with very low market shares, very limited profitability. For me, being new to the company, it was easy to see what the problem was. Our company was technology driven. We were very far from the consumer, especially in emerging markets.

For example, our operating model was that we would build the best product possible with our newest technology. This would take several years, and then after the product was developed, it was up to marketing to sell it. Sometimes, marketing wouldn't know anything about the new product until six months before it was introduced!

The way these new products got to emerging markets was that they were designed first for more-developed markets, sold there, and then after a few years, we would start selling them into emerging markets—where our experience was that they didn't sell very well. To turn this around, we needed to develop a product for low-income consumers, the kinds of consumers we saw in India and in other emerging markets. When I suggested this to my team, they said that the company had already done this, without success. I asked for more information.

Gillette had developed a razor called Vector specifically for the Indian market. It was not doing well, and customer feedback was very negative. For example, consumers complained that this razor got clogged with hair frequently, even though it used a plastic device on the product to make it easier to clean.

I asked, "How did you test this product?"

"We went to MIT in Cambridge, Massachusetts, where there are many Indian students, and we distributed a large number of these products. These Indian students then tested it and it got very high approval ratings. So, based on these very positive results, we decided to launch it in India. But it has never sold well."

Within a couple of weeks, I had booked a trip to India. I announced this to my entire management team: "I am going to India to spend a week observing how Indian men shave their beards."

This decision caused great turmoil in the company. "You are the president of this division. You shouldn't go. Leave it to us. We can send our people from R&D and market development." I told them, "No. I want to go there and see for myself how they shave their beards. Then I'll understand our market opportunities."

Naturally, after I decided to go, several people wanted to go with me. In the end, I had a big team with me during this trip—two people from R&D, two people from marketing, one person from engineering, one from product supply, two people from the development lab in the United Kingdom.

The people from the United Kingdom were particularly puzzled about the need for this trip to India. "We don't understand why you have to go all the way to India. There are so many Indians in London we can talk to."

I responded, "There is so much about India and how men shave there that we don't understand, and we will never understand if we only stay in London." So, off we went to India. We started reaching out to possible consumers, going to their homes at 5 a.m. to watch them shave and ask them key questions related to that moment. Most of these visits were in low-income areas.

What we found is that many of these low-income homes shared a single bathroom—maybe 30 or more homes shared one bathroom. So most of the men in these settings did not shave in this bathroom. Instead, they found rooms in their own home to shave, and most of these rooms didn't have any lights or running water. All they had was a tiny mirror hanging on the wall and a cup of water. They didn't even have a place to store their razors.

Obviously, these men could not afford to spend a great deal of money on their razors. But we kind of understood this. In fact, some people in engineering and finance told us that our trip to India would be futile: "There is no point going there. We know they need a cheaper product. We won't be able to make such a product. We don't have any platforms we can use to make such cheap products."

But it wasn't just the price of the product we were selling. Turns out we had the wrong product, no matter its price. Most of the Indian men who had tested our Vector product in the United States and in London shaved in their own bathroom with running water. So they could use the pressure from that running water to clean their razors. But many men in India did not have that luxury, and instead would shake their razor back and forth in a small cup of water to clean it. No wonder the Vector got clogged with hair so easily!

Men in the United States and the United Kingdom wanted a very close shave and therefore looked for a razor with several blades to get that benefit. Most men in India just wanted a shave to look good during the first part of the day. Also, the men in the United States and the United Kingdom usually had space to store their razors, often in the box in which they had been packaged and sold. The men in India didn't have that space. Instead, they hung their razor up on a small nail next to the mirror they used to shave. But the Vector didn't have a hole in the handle that could be used to hang it on the wall. Can you believe it? It didn't have a hole in the handle.

In short, because we did not understand how Indian men in India shaved, we did not understand the shaving product they needed. Because we didn't understand the product they needed, we tried to sell them the wrong product. And because we didn't think we could make a product that could compete on price, we tried selling them the wrong product at a high price. For all these reasons, we were failing in the Indian market. As important, we had no idea how big of an opportunity actually existed in that market.

On the way home from India, the team gathered on the airplane. First, we concluded that the opportunity in India—with the right product at the right price—would be huge! We then committed to design a new razor—only the essential parts, one blade, easy to clean even without running water, and with a hole in the handle—for one-third the cost of Gillette's cheapest razor. We needed to get the cost that low in order to get the retail price we needed in the market.

To cut a long story short, we began to develop and test a new razor that we would sell at a price point below any of the competitors in India. It was a huge success. In a couple of years, we went from almost 0 percent market share to 18 percent market share. Over 100 million Indian men bought this product in those first two years.

But this story was not just about selling more razors in India. It was about transforming the way products were developed at Gillette. The first trip we took to get closer to consumers caused great turmoil in the company. For our second trip, the majority of the people on the trip really wanted to engage in the process. By the third trip, people were seeing very tangible results, and they all wanted to collaborate. On this third trip to India, two VPs came along, each of whom had responsibility for a part of Gillette. They had never been so close to actual consumers where they had a chance to see those men shaving their beards.

Over time, I was asked to share this customer-centric approach to product development throughout the company. Of course, technological development is still important at Gillette. But now, developing an understanding of consumers and consumer preferences is the starting point.

Clearly, Alberto starred in his own story. Indeed, in another part of his interview, he observed, "We could have asked an intern to write a report describing how Indian men actually shaved. But that would probably not have had the impact of me and my team going to India and experiencing this for ourselves." For Alberto, culture change was not a spectator sport.

On the other hand, he could have gone to India by himself or with only a small group of people who already supported his ideas. Instead, he chose to go with much of his team, including several people who were skeptical about the entire undertaking. This was a risky choice on his part. After all, they could have gone to India and not made any useful discoveries about the Indian market and their products. It could have turned out to be a boondoggle. Like so many of the other culture-changing stories presented in this book, Alberto's story created vulnerability for him personally.

However, by taking his team with him, and especially by taking skeptics along, he was in the process of enabling a fundamental shift in Gillette's culture. They all came to understand the Indian consumer, and they all became agents for change when they returned home to face the skepticism of those who were still operating under the old technology-oriented culture. Ultimately, this first trip led to other trips, which led to further changes and developments until Gillette's culture was transformed.

Exemplifying the Culture

Concepts like values, beliefs, and norms—the building blocks of organizational culture—can be abstract and difficult to operationalize. You can say the words, but the meaning of those words—how they actually affect decision making in your organization—is not always clear. This is true if you are changing your organization's current culture or trying to build a culture for your organization from scratch.

This is another reason why business leaders need to star in the stories they build. Your employees watch what you do very closely—probably more closely than you imagine. When you engage in activities that exemplify what might otherwise be seen as abstract aspects of the culture, your employees see these actions, and they come to have a better understanding of the kind of culture you are trying to create.

Sure, other people in your organization could be engaging in such behaviors, and you can call attention to their culture-consistent actions as well. But the biggest impact on culture change is when you—the leader—engage in actions that exemplify the culture you are trying to create. Then people will take notice.

Jamie O'Banion—former model and founder of a successful skin care company—was literally the star in her company's marketing efforts. She personally went on televised shopping networks around the world to sell her company's skin care products. But the core values she was trying to incorporate into her company—truth, beauty, and empowerment—were fairly abstract, until her trip to the United Kingdom.

Story 4.5 "I Split My Eyebrow Wide Open"
Jamie O'Banion as CEO and founder at Beauty Biosciences LLC

I really grew up in the skin care industry that I'm in right now. My father is a physician. He was an anesthesiologist and became very interested in dermatology and biochemistry and became an owner, when I was very young, in one of the top skin care labs in the United States. I've always loved chemistry. I've always loved science. I loved spending time with my father at the lab, sitting behind a microscope and watching.

And then, in my late teens, one of my best friends entered me into the Miss Texas teen pageant. I didn't even know about it, but I ended up winning. That set me on a course of doing commercial print modeling for over a decade. During that time, I worked with the top makeup artists in the country on different photo shoots and was always asking them questions like, "Why are you using this cream?" and "What do you love about this product and these different techniques?"

So I came to the skin care industry with two very different skill sets—a deep interest in and love of the science of skin care, and practical experience in skin care I learned from these world-class makeup artists. With this background, I started BeautyBio. We launched BeautyBio with a focus on truth and beauty. There is a neon sign with those words in our main conference room—truth and beauty. And on the wall in the main entrance to our offices is another word that helps define our culture—empowerment. Everything in BeautyBio comes back to providing truth and beauty—we're really a brand focused on education. There is so much contradictory information about skin care today that to the extent we can credibly help consumers decipher this information and help them make informed choices, they will come to trust us, whether they were shopping for our brand or not. Truth and beauty make our customers and our employees empowered.

A big part of our business is on home shopping networks, like Home Shopping Network (HSN)—where we started—and now QVC (which acquired HSN). I represent the brand on these shows, and we've been very successful on them around the world. This can create insane travel challenges for me. In one particularly important trip, I went from Germany to the United Kingdom, to Italy, and to France in three days, with live television shows on all those days. We were launching on QVC in Germany—prime time, very important for us. Then I was off to QVC UK the next morning—a 24-hour show where I would be pitching our products every 2 hours for 24 hours.

I got back to the hotel at 10 p.m., had some other things I was working on, and looked at the clock—it was 1:04 a.m. The driver was coming to pick me up at 4:30 a.m., so I decided I needed to get some sleep.

So, I'm in my robe, rushing to make sure the front door of my suite is locked. The entryway into my room was pitch dark. I couldn't see anything, and I walked full speed into the edge of the partially ajar powder room door. I split my eyebrow wide open. As soon as it happened, I knew I would need sutures—blood was everywhere. But I'm going on live television later that day. To sell beauty products. With the giant gash in my eyebrow and what I imagined would be a black eye and a bruised face. My first thought was—I can't go on live television, selling skin care products, looking like I lost a prize fight!

But then the words we talk about at the company—truth, beauty, and empowerment—came to me. The truth is, bad stuff happens to people—we all run into actual or proverbial doors all the time. We all split open our eyebrows in life. But none of that affects our true underlying beauty. None of it changes our fundamental worth as human beings. Those ideas empowered me and made it okay for me to go on live television.

So the next day I simply put makeup on, took an eyebrow pencil and drew on top of the bandage over my brow, and swept my hair in a deep part to the side to cover that eye.

I talked about truth, and beauty, and empowerment—the fundamental themes of our company. And sure, that day, I didn't look like the classic spokesperson for our skin care brand. But I was modeling what our skin care brand stood for—truth, beauty, and empowerment. And sales went through the roof. Even today, whenever someone asks about what "truth, beauty, and empowerment" mean at BeautyBio, employees tell this story about how I split my eyebrow wide open and still sold beauty products on live television.

Conclusion

If you want to build a story that changes or creates your organizational culture, build a story in which you star. This is not because doing so gratifies your ego. It is because starring in your own story gives that story credibility. It empowers others to build their own stories, stories in which they also star. This, in turn, helps create a story cascade in your organization that, ultimately, changes your culture.

In the end, you cannot delegate the start of culture change. It must begin with you. However, by starring in your own story, you increase the chance that the story you are building will be seen as important, credible, and actionable. Our research shows that starring in your own story is one of the most important determinants of whether or not the story you are building will generate the cultural change you are seeking.

Consider another historical example.[1] Mohandas Gandhi was born October 2, 1869, in the coastal town of Porbandar, India. Educated as a lawyer in London, he moved with his wife and children to South Africa to practice his profession. After 21 years in South Africa—where he developed his methods of active nonviolence—he returned to India. There he became a leader in the Indian independence movement.

While in India, Gandhi engaged in a series of organized noncooperation campaigns. Taken as a whole, these campaigns had little effect on British policy toward India. By the mid-1920s, Gandhi was looking for another of these campaigns around which he could energize the Indian people.

During most of their rule in India, the British had a monopoly on the production and sale of salt. Not surprisingly, this vital substance was both expensive and in short supply—many of the poorest Indians could not obtain the salt they needed for a healthy diet. Gandhi decided to symbolically challenge this monopoly and in this way challenge the British rule of India.

To do so, he led a march from his home in Ahmedabad to the sea, at Dandi, Gujarat, where he would make salt in defiance of the British ban. He left with 78 volunteers on March 12, 1930—when he was 61 years old—on this 241-mile walk. As he walked, crowds began to join him. In the end, thousands joined him on the beach in Dandi, on April 6, to watch him make a small amount of salt.

The "salt march" of 1930 captured the imagination of millions of Indian citizens and is widely recognized for revitalizing the Indian independence movement. It brilliantly demonstrated the limitations of the British rule over India, and how active nonviolent noncooperation could highlight these limitations. Indian independence did not come for many years, but it did finally come. And Gandhi's march to the sea was an important turning point in this process.

Note, however, that, even at age 61, Gandhi walked the 241 miles to the sea. He averaged a bit more than 9 miles a day for 26 days. He did not ask someone to walk for him, although he asked many to walk with him. To build a story to help change how India was governed, Gandhi had to star in his own story.

To change your organizational culture, are you willing to "walk to the sea" in the same way as Gandhi?

CHAPTER FIVE

Stories That Break with the Past, with a Path toward the Future

The first two attributes of successful culture-change stories we identified—a story must be authentic, and it must star the business leader—have to do with the context and structure of a culture-changing story. The context is: it must reflect a business leader's true underlying values and beliefs. The structure is: it must star the business leader. We found no examples in our research of successful culture-changing stories that did not have these two essential attributes.

However, as important as the context and structure of the story are, the story you build to change your culture must also have content. Culture change is fundamentally about breaking well-entrenched patterns of thinking, acting, and responding and replacing them with new patterns. Thus, the stories you build to change your organization's culture have to make it clear what specific patterns of thinking, acting, and responding are no longer acceptable, and what these new patterns will be. That is, your story must identify a clear break with your cultural past and outline a path toward the new cultural patterns you think will be important going forward.

Getting Your Employees' Attention by Breaking with the Past

The values, norms, and beliefs that make up a culture can become so taken for granted in a firm that they become like habits. We behave in ways consistent with a culture because we can't even think about behaving in ways that are inconsistent with that culture. In the extreme, we may not even have a language to describe behavior that is inconsistent with a taken-for-granted culture.

In Story 4.4, for example, people at Gillette didn't have a language for product development that included developing a clear understanding of the consumer. It was never part of the conversation—until the first trip to India. In Story 1.1, senior managers at Telesp didn't know what customer service even meant, in practice, until they were forced to use the same service center as regular customers. And in Story 3.3, managerial transparency was largely unknown at this division in ADM until the new leader modeled an entirely new way of interacting with his colleagues.

Because behaving in ways that are consistent with an established culture can be habitual, even unconscious, one of the things that a culture-changing story must do is to get management's attention. It does this by making a clear statement that some aspects of the taken-for-granted culture will no longer be acceptable going forward.

Sometimes an attention-getting story can be built out of a small incident—as small as locking the door on a habitually late colleague.

STORY 5.1 "Senior Management Lockout"
Dennis Robinson as CEO at a major sports and entertainment venue

When I first started as CEO, one of my most senior management staff members was a functional expert but not a good leader or communicator. He always had an edge, and was regularly and unnecessarily argumentative, always contradicting people, and not listening. To make matters worse, he was always late—it seemed that he wanted to be late to force his people to wait for him. I think he thought walking in late let his people know who was in charge.

Not surprisingly, his people were not happy. I knew I had to work with him on his leadership and listening skills as well as emotional intelligence. I decided to start with his being on time. I told him, "My expectation is that everyone will be on time for meetings. If you've got 10 people at a meeting, and you are 5 minutes late, you're being disrespectful and you've just wasted 50 minutes of your colleagues' time." He agreed to be on time.

So, it's the first meeting of the year. It starts at 9 a.m., and he isn't there. I closed the door, locked it, and started the meeting. About 5 or 10 minutes later, there's a knock on the door. Someone says, "That's got to be . . ." I said, "Yeah. Probably is. Let's keep going." We continued the meeting for about 10 minutes, while he was waiting in the hall. Finally, I opened the door and let him in. Everyone looked around the table with wide eyes, but I didn't say a word. He sat down, and we continued the meeting. It was the last time he was late.

So, I have a simple saying when it comes to building a leadership team: "No jerks allowed." I told my people, "We're here to work together to solve problems. I want your best thinking. I want you to disagree, but we want to do it in a way that is collaborative, respectful, where people will listen and learn from each other. And I want you to enjoy your work and the people you work with." I said this to them straight out, "If you can't operate this way, then you should find someplace else to work." I said it as simple as that. In the end, we had a wonderful and dedicated senior management team and pulled off the world's greatest events.

We suspect that few people were ever again late to one of Dennis's meetings. The simple act of locking the door demonstrated a clear break with the past and hinted at a path to the future—a future where employees valued each other's time.

Providing a Path to the Future

Given how this and the other stories we have already seen create such a clear break with the past suggests why sometimes culture change is so difficult. Of course, some of your employees will see the cultural changes you are suggesting as a breath of fresh air.

Many more will look at you like you have a hole in your head.

For this latter group of employees, what you are suggesting is nothing less than blowing up the way they have worked together for years. You are asking them to take out their old brain and put a new brain in. That is just as painful as it sounds.

For this reason, it is usually not enough that your story breaks with the past—although this is essential. Your story also has to show a path to the future. As we will see, this doesn't mean that you have to have this future all worked out in detail before you start changing the culture. Indeed, if you work out too many of the details of this cultural future ahead of time, you are essentially eliminating the opportunity for your employees to cocreate this future with you. This cocreation process helps people understand the new culture that is being created and increases their commitment to the new culture they are helping to create.

An impactful culture-change story balances the need to break with the past with the need to point to a path toward the future—without predetermining too much of that future culture. Balancing these elements of a culture-changing story can be difficult, but consider the following examples.

Building Our New Customer Delight Culture Together

STORY 5.2 "Learning to Delight the Consumer"
Melanie Healey as vice president and general manager,
North America Feminine Care at Procter & Gamble

I was the first woman asked to head up P&G's feminine care business in North America. The business had been in trouble. Sales and profit were meaningfully down for some time, and I was asked to turn this around. One of my many observations coming into this role was that not only did the team lack gender and ethnic diversity, but it was also very focused on the functional aspect of the product and not as focused on the comfort, feel, and design of the product. It was clear to me that we had lost our passion for serving our consumers' needs and wants.

The first thing we did was change up the team to be more diverse, more in touch with the consumer and their desires for products and experiences that not only performed better but that made them feel valued. I considered this almost a calling—it was my mission to make women's experiences with our products better, to the point that our products would delight our consumers. We needed to help make the passage from being a girl to being a woman a positive event in their lives, much like how boys feel when they first shave. If we did this right, women could be more self-confident and feel more empowered to conquer anything in their lives. This became my purpose and mission and the key was to inspire the organization to feel the same way.

And so, the journey began. Our first step was to dig into all the research and data in house. We also spent a ton of time with consumers aged 12 to 55 to understand their needs, wants, and desires for an ideal product. Our goal was to create products that not only worked but also delighted women. One of my favorite examples I'd use to inspire our folks was J&J's Sesame Street Band-Aids. If a kid fell down and grazed his knee and all you had was a standard Band-Aid, chances are they would keep on crying. You had resolved the functional aspect of that situation but not the emotional side. Only a Sesame Street Band-Aid had that power. So I began asking, where was the Sesame Street effect in our products?

One of the exercises we did with our team together with consumers was to lay out examples of our products, our competitive products, and other categories that had not just embraced the functional attributes of a product but also the design elements. It was clear to all of us that when we went around the table, the products that everyone wanted more of were those that not only worked but importantly made them feel better about using them. That exercise really helped our team understand the importance of bringing that aspect of everyday delight to our products not only at the "second moment of truth" (which is when you use the product), but also at the "first moment of truth" (when you buy the product).

Next was to re-create our innovation program. Again, there was no doubt that our products worked better than our competition. Our team had nailed that years ago. The goal now was to also step-change the design of our products so that they would truly delight women around the world. It was this effort that led to significantly better packaging, beautiful wrappers for our product, and new functional design elements like the blue core, the Always Infinity technology (first of its kind in the category) where we created a technology that not only absorbed 10 times its weight but was also delightfully comfortable to wear.

We also created a new plastic applicator called Tampax Pearl to compete with Playtex. This was the first innovation that incorporated all our functional design–focused efforts. For example, pearls became an inspirational element for a new design for our Tampax applicator. Pearls are smooth. They are beautiful. If you looked at our Tampax applicator at the time, it was made out of cardboard. There is probably nothing more uncomfortable than having to use a tampon with a cardboard applicator. The pearl was the inspiration for making a smoother, gentler applicator.

In fact, everything we did with this product focused on delighting our customers. Instead of putting the product in a box that was sometimes hard to open, our new package opened like a purse. And instead of making a loud ripping sound when the wrapper was opened, we designed a silent wrapper. Tampax Pearl became the market leader within five years of launch.

The team was ecstatic with the results and from then on, the mission of making a difference in women's lives by providing them with products they loved to use every day and everywhere became the new mantra not just for North America but globally.

The results were remarkable. We already had 50 percent market share in the pad market in North America with Always. Within six years, we got to a 60 percent share with Always and finally leadership in the tampon plastic applicator market. We grew two share points every year during those years. We had made numerous attempts to grow our Tampax share with our cardboard product, but they had all failed until we changed our culture to one that was truly focused on delighting our consumers.

Melanie added that her biggest learnings during those years were:

(1) Focus on your consumer and what they want or need. Sometimes we let our internal assets drive our innovations because it's more efficient that way. That's never enough. The consumer is boss, and your goal is to meet her needs better than anyone else.

(2) Having a clear vision and purpose is critical for any leader wanting to transform a business. Embracing the purpose of delighting women with products that truly delighted them and made them feel like a woman became not only her purpose but everyone's purpose in feminine care. It was contagious, energizing, and inspiring to see that come to life in their culture.

(3) Ensure that your purpose and vision are transformed to business results too. Understand clearly what your sources of growth opportunity are and then hardwire your plans to deliver innovations and commercial plans that go after those sources of growth. She said up front that their goal was to grow two share points each year and they had clear and compelling sources of growth for that share growth.

(4) Surround yourself with the most diverse, collaborative, smart, and passionate team of leaders. It takes a diverse, inspired, and energized group of people to make meaningful changes in our world.

When Melanie brought her managers together to watch customers sort products into more and less delightful categories, she was building a powerful story about how the feminine care products business at P&G needed to break from the past—a cultural past that emphasized manufacturing efficiency and product effectiveness but not "delighting" the customer. As important, designing new products that emulated the smoothness of pearls helped her managers see a path to the future—toward a culture where feminine hygiene products were not just functional but were empowering to women. And the financial results of building a culture to enable the implementation of these new product strategies speak for themselves.

Of course, if Melanie had just stood up in front of her top management team and preached the importance of delighting their customers, they would have been confused. It would have been like someone speaking to them in a language they did not understand. To those who grew up in the old culture, such a sermon would have sounded like the gibberish ravings of a lunatic. This would have been the case even though Melanie's view of the business built on a motivating, even inspirational, purpose—to help women become more comfortable and confident in all aspects of their lives. But this was a foreign language to those who knew and had been successful in the old culture.

She needed to build a culture-changing story that identified a clear break with the past and also described a cultural path forward.

Building a Path to the Future by Looking to the Past

Melanie Healey had an important advantage in changing the culture at the feminine care products division at P&G: the company had developed some valuable manufacturing skills and was successful in at least some of its markets. What her culture-change story could do was help her managers see that the company could build on its traditional strengths and be even more successful. Once they became aware of the limitations of their manufacturing culture, they could see how they could leverage the great parts of that culture in developing, manufacturing, and selling products that delighted their consumers.

Ivan Filho faced an even more difficult situation as a business unit manager at Tenneco. Located in England, Tenneco had a strong union and a history of antagonism between management and labor. Ivan had to build a series of stories to completely change the culture in this business unit, or it would probably have folded. And these stories had to mark a clear break with the past, while also defining a path to the future. That future turned out to be related to something deep in this division's history—the Battle of Britain during the Second World War.

Story 5.3 "Rediscovering the Spirit of the Spitfire"
Ivan Sartori Filho as York production and business
unit manager at Tenneco

Tenneco had recently purchased the business unit where I was assigned as the production manager. We manufactured automobile parts that were supplied to various car manufacturers in Europe. Because it was recently acquired, this business unit had a culture that was separate from the rest of the corporation. In fact, managers in the business unit were responding with difficulty to their new American owners. Their mindset could be summarized in three sentences: "I'm the one who is knowledgeable here." "There's only one way to work, and we know what that way is." "We don't need anyone telling us what to do."

The managers and employees all believed these things, and yet the business unit was not performing well.

So, here I arrive, and my job is to turn this business unit around or get ready to close it. I was supposed to start on a Monday, but I like to go early and visit the places where I am going to work, just to get a lay of the land. So I went to the factory on Saturday. To my surprise, I found many employees working on Saturday. It was late Saturday afternoon, and they were all working overtime. Almost all the production lines were still operating. The company's numbers certainly did not justify the need to have all those people working overtime, but despite this, most of the staff was there.

As I walked in the front door, down toward the production area, one of the employees left the production area and blocked my progress.

"Are you the new sheriff here?" he asked.

"I'm sorry, but I don't think that is my position title," I replied.

He narrowed his stare at me. "When we first found out you were joining the company, we made a bet between us about how long you would last here. Our bet was that you wouldn't last three months. But now that I've had a chance to meet you, to see you face to face, I've changed my mind. I think you'll last just one month."

I tried to not get too defensive. "It's actually been a pleasure to meet you. From what I can tell, we have lots to do here. We're going to have to change many things—not the least your assumption about how long I'm going to work here. I'm really counting on your help so we can make all these changes together. Now, if you'll excuse me, I need to go to the factory so I can continue my evaluation."

Turns out this guy was the president of the trade union. I had to go through many tough moments with this man, but when I eventually left the company, I am happy to say that many employees, including the leadership of the trade union, signed a very nice card for me, wishing me well. And this trade union president delivered the card to me personally.

When I got to the plant on Monday, I heard the same line time after time: "Here, the directors and the leaders do the thinking, the foremen do the talking, and everyone else does the doing." I knew I would have to try to break this culture down if we were going to be able to turn the business around.

Not surprisingly, the company was also very siloed. Even though different functions—assembly, production, technology, and engineering—all operated in the same location, they hardly ever communicated with each other. They were like separate little fiefdoms. There was great resistance to communicating among these functions, so things didn't happen in an integrated way. Instead, each manager protected their own unit.

The same sort of communication barriers existed with our customers. We didn't understand what they needed. None of our operational areas had a clue who the company's clients were. None of them had ever visited the clients' locations.

The business was not open or transparent at all. Operating results were guarded as if they were secret. Whenever operating information did reach the different functional areas, it was always accompanied by some criticism—"You are not doing your work properly," or "It's your fault that we didn't get products delivered on time," or "Your functional area is responsible for our poor performance." Information was shared to accuse operational areas of poor performance and not as a way to solve problems and make things better. This made the different operating units in the company even more distant, even less willing to work together.

But this was just the way things were done in this organization. It was just taken for granted. No one even thought about doing business differently.

It had not always been this way at this plant. In fact, during World War II, this had been one of several plants that manufactured the Spitfire airplanes that were so important for England's survival—airplanes that were instrumental in winning the war. The parents of many of the people who currently worked in this plant had been part of that effort. They were justifiably proud of this heritage.

During the dark days at the beginning of the war, this plant built enough planes to turn the tide of the Battle of Britain. There was a spirit of dedication and cooperation during those days that people in the plant still talked about. In fact, most of our employees were the children and grandchildren of those heroic workers. I felt honored to work at such a sacred place.

I built on this history as I began to try to change the culture of the plant. I proposed that we turn the business around using the same spirit that enabled their fathers and grandfathers, mothers and grandmothers, to be part of a great victory in World War II. We needed to create a more integrated team, to break down communication barriers. We had to have a common purpose, to realize that the enemy was not our fellow employees, or our clients, or even me.

Once, when I found out that one of our employees was injured on the job, I went over to his house to visit him. I wanted to see what was happening and how I could help him and his family. At the time, people in the business were really surprised that I did this. They would say: "We don't understand what's going on. . . . Our leader went to visit him at his house. . . ." Not just hourly employees were saying this. Some of our senior managers did as well. To me, I was just trying to break down the hierarchy, to show that we all had more in common than we had differences.

I also changed where we held leadership meetings. Instead of offsite, we now met within the factory's grounds. And during those meetings, everyone remained standing in the midst of the assembly machines. People who worked in particular production units would come to meetings in their areas, to share their ideas for improvement. In this way, these employees were not just "doing the doing," they were doing the talking and the thinking too.

We did this for nonproduction units as well. Management would meet in a particular unit, find out what it was like to work in those units, and this helped create a common understanding that helped break down the communication barriers. In those meetings, we kept asking the same question: "How can we contribute to your success?"

This question became a very important part of our culture, not just with each other but with our clients. Whenever an issue emerged between different operating units, the key question that was asked was "How can we contribute to your success?" Both units would ask this question, and then cooperation was possible. And then we started asking all our customers the same thing: "How can we contribute to your success?"

We were very proud of our performance. Within a year, our business unit was operating as efficiently as any other business unit in Europe. Those other business units used to be our role models; now they started visiting our operations regularly, so we could show our best practices to them.

So, not only had we avoided lots of job cuts in this business unit, but we became a well-respected operation in the corporation. We were all proud of these achievements.

I think we all felt a little like we were building Spitfires again.

Ivan's stories helped his business unit break with the past and also showed a path to the future. Notice, however, that Ivan did not reject everything from the past. Like Melanie Healey in the feminine hygiene product example, Ivan took some of the best elements of this firm's history—namely, the role it played in defending Great Britain during World War II—and tried to build on these elements as the culture of the place was transformed.

Breaking with the Past Often Creates Conflict

Another thing the stories in this chapter have in common is that building stories that break from the past often creates conflict with those who have an interest or preference to maintain the past. To break with the past required Dennis Robinson (Story 5.1) to lock his CFO out of a meeting. For Melanie Healey at P&G (Story 5.2), building a culture that focused on delighting customers was seen by at least some managers as putting the company's traditional focus on efficient manufacturing at risk. As for Ivan Filho at Tenneco (Story 5.3), entrenched interests in the union and among managers led to some tough confrontations as a new culture was being created.

These kinds of conflicts and confrontations are virtually inevitable in culture change. How a leader responds to these challenges can be an important source of culture-changing stories. This was certainly the case for Michael Speigl when he was still a relatively young manager in the car retailing business.

Story 5.4 "Working 36 Hours Straight"
Michael Speigl as general sales manager at Cox Automotive

From the very beginning of my career, I knew what I wanted to do—I wanted to own and operate car dealerships. So, even if my job was, say, in the finance department, I spent time learning the sales function in a dealership. And when I was in sales, I spent time over in the service department learning how to sell service, how to turn service into new car sales. I went to used car auctions even when I wasn't in the used car part of the firm, and so on.

This approach had two effects on me. First, I came to understand how important it was for everyone in a dealership to learn how to cooperate in making money for the business. Sometimes we made money through financing, sometimes through the sale price of a car, sometimes on the trade-in, sometimes on service, sometimes on all these aspects of the business. No one function in a dealership was more important than any other—we all needed to work together to make money. Teamwork was essential for the success of a dealership.

Second, because I was trained in all the different parts of operating a dealership, I had the opportunity to become a general manager at a relatively young age—I took over running two dealerships when I was 27 years old. I know I was young, and in retrospect, I shouldn't have been surprised when some employees began testing me, testing my commitment to the cooperative organizational culture I was preaching.

What happened was that two senior people in the finance group basically tried to hold me hostage. They came to my office and said, "Hey, we're backed up and we've got all these deals we need to get done, and we're never going to get them all done in the current situation. To make sense for us to get all these deals done in a timely way, we are going to need a substantial raise." And the raise they had in mind was outrageous. "So," they continued, "we want this raise and if we don't get it, we're going to have to find work elsewhere."

I immediately took them up on their offer to walk out if I didn't meet their demands. I said, "Well, we had a contract for you to work for X, and if you don't want to work for the contract that we have, then by all means I respect your decision to leave." I think they were a little shocked by that, because, after all, they were basically the entire finance department. They currently had something like 40 deals to process. All the paperwork for these deals needed to be completed, packaged together, sent off to the bank, and so forth. This department probably needed at least three people. Two people was pretty tight—which is why they were behind—but now we would have no one in the department.

But remember, before I became a general manager, I had spent some time in several finance departments. So I took their 40 deals, organized them on my desk, and completed all the required work. To do it, I had to work 36 hours straight. I didn't go home for 36 hours. I had people bringing me food. My wife, who was my girlfriend at the time, asked that I text her pictures of myself throughout the night, to see that I was okay. I remember every hour on the hour I would text her a picture of the clock and myself.

Keep in mind, when we had new customers, I then had to stop, move these old deals to the side and do a brand-new fresh transaction with a new customer, and then add that deal to the pile. So, for two days I took all the fresh deals that came in, while cleaning up the 40 deals we were behind on.

I finally went home at like ten or eleven o'clock that next night, and for that next week I did every single deal myself. No other help. No other personnel. In addition to running both of those stores. So, I acted as the entire finance department and the general sales manager of both those stores for about a week and a half. Then I hired one person who was my partner and teammate. Then we hired another person, and I could remove myself from the finance department. Then we hired a third person, and that's how we built the core of the sustainable finance department that lasted for years.

That week of taking over the entire finance department and not being held hostage by those two employees, and specifically those 36 hours where I didn't leave that desk, was a story that was told time and time again. Really, I've carried it with me my entire career.

People ask me why I did such a crazy thing. To me, it wasn't a hard decision. I knew the kind of organization I wanted—one that focused on cooperation and teamwork across the various departments. And I knew that what these guys were doing was deeply inconsistent with that objective. I

> couldn't give in to that kind of blackmail, not even a little, and not even for a short period of time. That would have undermined the kind of culture I was trying to build.
>
> So, working 36 hours straight was what helped me build those first two dealerships into the financial successes they became. And that story—because it stuck with me—helped me build other successful dealerships throughout my career. Those 36 hours were probably the best investment in my career that I ever made.

Clearly, Michael had the courage of his convictions. He knew the kind of organizational culture he wanted to create in his business. And he knew why that organizational culture would create economic value. He discovered, however, that breaking with the past meant creating—and confronting—conflict. He could not compromise with this conflict even if that meant working 36 hours straight.

Michael's experience tells us something else about culture-changing stories. When you build an authentic story, in which you star, that clearly breaks with the past and points a path to the future, that story can stick with you. Even if you change companies, you can sometimes still be known as "the guy who worked for 36 hours straight"—in Michael's case—or "the woman who visited the barges in New Orleans"—in Annette Friskopp's case (Story 4.1). In these settings, building a story not only has an impact on the culture of your current firm, it can have an impact on the culture of future firms as well.

Breaking Down the Walls in a Siloed Culture

Michael Speigl had to stand up against two employees who tried to take advantage of him. All he had to do was to work 36 hours straight to make it clear to everyone, for the rest of his career, that such behavior was unacceptable in his companies.

But the scale of resistance to cultural change can be much larger than just a couple of employees who want a new contract. In these situations, building one culture-changing story will rarely be enough to actually change an organization's culture. Consider the example of a business leader who was asked to turn around a company with an iconic brand, a company that had become siloed and bloated with cost.

STORY 5.5 "Changing the Culture of a Traditional Industry Leader"
The CEO of a global corporation

I was asked to take over as CEO of a very well-known American firm that had just been purchased by a global company. I knew the day I took this job that I faced the greatest culture-change challenge of my career.

This company was an icon in its industry. It was over 100 years old, had a very well-known brand both in the United States and around the world, and was the sales leader in many of its markets. But it was more than just its brand and its sales.

This company was—at least in my mind—the best. I had visited their headquarters many times. They were always my reference point for what a great company in this segment could look like. They had beautiful buildings and amazing modern automated factories. An earlier CEO had provided steady leadership in the company for many, many years. From a practical point of view, he had created a state-of-the-art company worldwide.

But when the most recent CEO took over, the company began to lose its way. Or maybe, it had been losing its way for some time, and the problems only then became obvious.

By the time I got there, the company had developed a very formal, hierarchical culture. Very siloed. It also had a culture that didn't pay much attention to costs. The result was that while the company had a very strong brand name and was well established in its markets, it was oversized, too costly in most of its businesses, and deeply risk-averse.

And here I am, coming in from outside the company. And I was charged with the responsibility of changing this costly organizational culture.

We already knew how to reduce costs—the global firm had a playbook for this. After just a few weeks, we laid off hundreds of salaried employees, decided to not fill over 200 open positions, and eliminated several contractor jobs. Buyouts had been offered to employees just before the acquisition was completed, and 1,000 employees—including most of the company's senior management team—took them, or there would have been even more layoffs. We also instituted smaller but symbolically important changes: We asked employees to use both sides of copy paper, to stay in standard rather than luxury hotels when traveling on business, to fly on discount airlines rather than in first class. We also reduced the number of advertising firms with whom we worked and cut down on some marketing events. Again, in these efforts, we were just implementing a cost-reducing game plan that the global company had used in its other acquisitions.

Changing the formal, siloed, and hierarchical culture was harder. The company's building was large, and everybody had their own offices. My office was a huge corner office. My secretary's office was bigger than my meeting room at the global company where I had had a very senior position. The executive team had its own cafeteria. They wouldn't eat with the workers. We decided to change that. I started eating with the workers. I got to know the cooks—I'd give them a big hug when I saw them. Once, when we were having a reception at a home owned by the company, I saw one of the cafeteria attendants working. I went up to him and gave him a big hug, thanked him for working for us. We chatted for a while. I wanted to treat all our employees the same, with the same respect.

I could sense that all the managers in the room were thinking the same thing—"What's going on? Why is the CEO hugging the cafeteria attendant?"

Shortly after that, I was wondering how we could break down the walls between the functional groups in the company. I kept saying to myself—how do we break down these walls, how do we break down these walls? And then it occurred to me that we needed to literally break down some walls.

Each of these managers used to be in a private office. After a couple of months, I moved them all to a large space, a space with no walls. They couldn't stay in their offices and hide. Everyone could see when they came in in the morning and how late they stayed at night. If you needed to talk to someone, you could see them and go talk to them.

And yes, I had space in that big room as well.

Of course, it took some time to change the culture of this big company, but the results were very positive. Despite the financial difficulties of recent years, within a year, we had cut our expenses by a third, we had sold noncore assets worth billions of dollars, and had refinanced our heavy debt load on much more favorable terms. Our profit margins were up, as were our total profits. We felt that we had put this American icon into a great position for long-term success.

This leader's focus on cost containment was an essential part of the company's long-term financial success. Each of these cost-cutting acts, we are sure, built culture-changing stories. But developing respect for all of this firm's employees and breaking down the silos that had developed throughout the company were, if anything, more challenging cultural changes than enacting cost controls. Eating with regular employees, visibly connecting with the cafeteria workers, and tearing down the office walls were the kinds of acts that built powerful culture-changing stories. And this culture change was one of the reasons why this company's performance began to improve.

Coming Back from the Brink

Even though this organization may have lost its way before the new CEO took over, it still had a strong brand and deep market penetration. This CEO knew that if he could get the culture right, he would be able to take advantage of these strengths to rebuild a successful company. That was not the case when DaVita—a company that provides kidney dialysis services—began its cultural transformation. It was emerging from bankruptcy.

> **STORY 5.6 "We Needed to Cross a Bridge"**
> **Mike Staffieri as COO at DaVita**
>
> I joined DaVita in the early 2000s, just after the company was beginning its turnaround. We almost had to declare bankruptcy in the late 1990s, when we were known as Total Renal Care. But in the summer of 2000, after Kent Thiry took over as CEO, we changed the name of the company to DaVita—Italian for "to give life"—and began our turnaround.
>
> And we needed a turnaround. We weren't just financially bankrupt; we were culturally bankrupt. We had no purpose, no sense of direction. And this was a company that provided lifesaving kidney dialysis services to thousands and thousands of people each day. If we failed in our purpose, people could die.
>
> Morale was in the toilet. Just lots of unhappy and grumpy people. In these settings, if you try to do a big rah-rah meeting announcing a "culture change," lots of people are skeptical. They just sit there and say, "I don't believe you. I don't think the cultural changes you are trying to make are real." It's hard to build momentum for cultural change if too many people are going to say, "Hey, I'm going to sit and wait on the sidelines."

So we created this symbol of a bridge. We talked about it at every meeting and said, "Look, we want to build a special place, a special company. And if too many people just sit on the sidelines and won't cross the bridge and be part of making this happen, it will never happen. One CEO can't make it happen. One COO can't make it happen. If, on the other hand, lots of people begin to have hope and excitement about creating a special place, then it will happen."

And so, at every meeting, we talked about what we called an "inescapable decision"—are you going to be one of the people who makes this organization special or are you going to wait and see? And when you cross over from being "wait and see" to "making it happen," it's like crossing a bridge. We didn't know for sure, exactly, what we would be doing differently in this new culture and organization, but if we had a positive intent in "crossing that bridge" good things would start to happen.

Early on, we would set up actual bridges in big meetings. To get into the meeting, you could choose—if you wanted—to cross a bridge. On the far end of the bridge was a bucket that held coins—specially designed coins that talked about DaVita and what we wanted to stand for. When you were mentally prepared to do so, you would cross this bridge and grab a coin out of the bucket and take it back to your office, clinic, or wherever you were working. It was a way of saying, just to yourself, "I'm in. I'm not going to be on the sidelines. I'm going to be one of the leaders at DaVita that is going to make things happen." And that coin on my desk was a reminder of that commitment.

Even today, everywhere you go in DaVita, you will see images of bridges to remind us of this early commitment.

Since this cultural turnaround, DaVita has become financially successful and a leader in the dialysis industry.

DaVita's cultural change is particularly instructive. First, notice that the new COO invited his employees to join in the culture change by "crossing a bridge." He anticipated the skepticism that often accompanies flashy announcements of a new culture and did not try to coerce people to become part of the change; he waited until they were ready. Probably some people were never ready to engage in this change, and presumably those people left the firm. But over time, "crossing the bridge" built momentum for culture change.

Second, the details of this new culture were not spelled out by senior managers or a culture-change specialist. There was no list of "core values" or "cultural imperatives" that were announced by senior management, with the obligatory genuflection by less senior managers. Rather, DaVita's management asked its employees to cocreate this new culture with them. When they "crossed the bridge" together, their only commitment was to make this a special organization, a place where "good things could happen."

Third, DaVita's management used symbols of this cultural change to represent and dramatize this change. These symbols were simple—a bridge, a coin—yet carried a powerful message: We are not going to be what we have been. We are going to cross a bridge and never turn back.

Conclusion

Building stories that break with the past while establishing a path to the future can be difficult because often it is hard to give up the past. The past sometimes leaks into the future and makes the path to realize a new cultural future difficult.

Suppose, for example, that the engineering function was more valued than the marketing function in your old culture. You may want the marketing function to be more prominent in your culture going forward, but given your historical emphasis on engineering, do you really have the people you need to make marketing more prominent in your firm? Also, suppose that US operations have been more valued in your old culture than operations in other geographic regions. You may want to change this in your culture going forward, but in emphasizing operations in new markets, do you really want to jeopardize operations in historically dominant US markets? These are examples of ways that your past cultural values can leak into efforts to create new cultural values.

One time in history where this difficult relationship between the cultural past and the cultural future was especially notable occurred in South Africa as that nation was emerging from decades of racist apartheid policies. Postapartheid South Africa was trying to build a culture where all races and ethnicities were valued equally. But how could this be done when the abuses of the country's apartheid past—only a few years earlier—had been so heinous?[1]

This task was what Nelson Mandela inherited when he became the first democratically elected Black president of South Africa in 1994.[2]

Trained as a lawyer, Mandela had become involved in the movement to overthrow apartheid when he was in his 20s. Early in his activist career, Mandela had subscribed to the nonviolent approaches preached by Gandhi.[3] However, later on, he led a sabotage conspiracy against the government. As a result, in 1962, he was convicted of trying to overthrow the state and sentenced to life in prison.

Mandela was imprisoned for 27 years. He was released by South African president F. W. de Klerk in 1990 and subsequently, with de Klerk, negotiated an end to apartheid. The first multiracial general election in South African history was finally held in 1994, and the African National Congress (ANC) came into power. Mandela—who had led the ANC since shortly after being released from prison—became South Africa's first Black president.

One of the first issues that Mandela had to decide was how to address South Africa's racist apartheid past in a way that made the development of a new multiracial culture in South Africa's future possible. Some members of the ANC—including Mandela's estranged wife—wanted to use the ANC's newly acquired power to identify and punish members of the government and police officers who had helped enforce apartheid. Other parts of South African society—especially South African whites—wanted to ignore their country's apartheid past and instead focus on building its multiracial future.

Mandela could not be convinced by either of these extreme points of view. On the one hand, he was concerned that taking retribution on members of the South African government and police forces would terrify many South African whites, many of whom would then emigrate. This would deprive South Africa of much of the managerial and technical talent that was essential for its continued economic success. Mandela had already seen this occur in other African countries that had recently eliminated minority white rule.[4]

On the other hand, ignoring the human rights abuses of the apartheid rule would have been disrespectful to the hundreds of thousands of South Africa's Black citizens who had suffered so severely during those dark and painful years.

To break with the past while building a path to the future, Mandela created the Truth and Reconciliation Commission (TRC). Formed in 1996 and chaired by Archbishop Desmond Tutu (a well-respected cleric who had played a significant role in destroying apartheid), the purposes of the TRC were to offer individuals who had suffered gross human rights abuses under apartheid an opportunity to give statements about what they had suffered, and to give perpetrators of these abuses an opportunity to make statements about their role in these events and to request amnesty from both civil and criminal prosecution. In total, 22,025 gross human rights violations that had occurred between 1960 and 1994 were reported to the TRC. In addition, 7,111 amnesty applications were submitted to the TRC, but only 849 were granted.[5]

Many—but certainly not all—observers believed that the TRC was useful in (1) confirming the abuses that had occurred during apartheid, (2) creating a sense of reconciliation between Blacks and whites in South Africa, and (3) helping South Africa regain its status as a respected nation internationally while continuing to grow its economy internally.[6] Mandela summarized the impact of the TRC more simply: "Courageous people do not fear forgiving, for the sake of peace."[7]

Mandela also used other powerful symbols to build stories about the importance of creating a multiracial culture in South Africa. For example, South Africa's national sport is rugby. Its national team, the Springboks, had historically been all-white and had become a hated symbol of apartheid among many South African Blacks. In 1995, the Rugby World Cup was held in South Africa, and—just after apartheid had been officially rejected as South Africa's racial policy—the Springboks included one Black player on their squad.

Mandela saw the opportunity to use South Africa's obsession with rugby, and the Springboks' admittedly modest attempt at integration, to unite the country behind a new multiracial culture.

So, at the Cup final against New Zealand, Mandela wore a Springbok jersey.

He wore this jersey at a time when it was still widely hated by many South African Blacks as a symbol of apartheid. But he wore it as a symbol of both breaking with the past and building a new future in South Africa.[8]

Of course, many people have been critical of Mandela's approach. Some have argued that he was too conciliatory to South African whites, that he focused too much on negotiating with the whites and not enough on securing economic rights for South African Blacks. Others have argued that he was too focused on Black rights in ways that led to the emigration of many whites from South Africa.[9]

All that said, it is fairly clear that Mandela consciously focused on finding a way to break with South Africa's racist cultural past but in a way that also pointed to its multiracial cultural future. Apparently, the Nobel Committee approved of these efforts, and Nelson Mandela—after languishing in prison for 27 years—was awarded the Nobel Peace Prize in 1993.

Are you ready to build stories that break with your organization's cultural past and provide a path to your organization's cultural future?

CHAPTER SIX

Build Stories for the Head and Heart

We saw in the last chapter that stories that are built to change an organization's culture must have content that signals a clear break with a firm's cultural past and a path toward its cultural future. We saw how simple incidents—like locking the CFO out of a meeting—can generate these effects. We also saw that more elaborate actions—like having customers sort products at the feminine care business at P&G or breaking down hierarchy and silos at Tenneco—can have these same cultural effects.

However, our research also found that these stories need an additional content element if they are to be successful in changing an organization's culture. These stories must appeal to your employees' heads and to their hearts. Your stories appeal to your employees' heads when they draw a direct causal line between the new culture you are trying to create and your firm's financial performance. They appeal to your employees' hearts when they see how a new culture will benefit people associated with your company—people about whom they care, including coworkers, subordinates, and customers. Appealing to your employees' heads is about rationality and economics; appealing to their hearts is about emotions, loyalty, and personal relationships.

Why Both Heads and Hearts?

People tend to have mixed reactions when we talk about heads and hearts in building culture-changing stories. Some are confused by—and perhaps personally uncomfortable with—the affective dimensions of culture change. These people reason: "Isn't the purpose of organizations of all types, including public and private for-profit firms as well as not-for-profit firms, to create sufficient economic value to compensate their critical stakeholders for investing their time and treasure in these organizations?"

The answer to this question is, of course, "Yes."

So, if almost all organizations need to focus on creating enough economic value to compensate their stakeholders for investing in them, why do culture-changing stories need to appeal both to your employees' heads and hearts? Wouldn't it be enough to demonstrate—through the stories you build—that the new culture you are cocreating is going to generate economic value that will benefit your employees and your other stakeholders? Why all this emphasis on trust and friendship and teamwork and the emotions that are associated with these affective dimensions of organizations?

Of course, the answer to this question is that organizational cultures are, at their core, social in nature. They exist because your employees have come to accept certain values, beliefs, and norms of behavior that define what are, and what are not, culturally consistent ways of interacting with each other. Changing these values, beliefs, and norms is not just a matter of rational calculation, it is a matter of changing the way that your employees think about themselves and their relationships with each other. To make these kinds of changes, your employees must be engaged in culture change, not just intellectually and rationally but in a deeply emotional and personal way.

Of course, focusing only on the "heart" portion of culture change can be just as problematic as focusing only on the "head." After all, the point of changing an organization's culture is to do so in a way that enhances your organization's ability to implement its new strategies. If culture change helps everyone in an organization get along with each other, but getting along with each other does not create economic value, then this kind of culture change is difficult to justify economically. Culture change that focuses only on the heart is easy to interpret as a manifestation of a leader's ego, rather than an attempt to create a more effective and efficient organization.

The Tension between Head and Heart in Culture Change

So, changing organizational cultures must involve both the head and the heart. But aren't these elements of culture change—to some extent, at least—antithetical? Well, there certainly can be tension between rational economic reasons for changing an organization's culture and emotional and interpersonal reasons to do so. But skilled leaders can build stories that appeal both to their employees' heads and hearts. Sometimes they alternate between head and heart reasons for culture change.

Alternating between the Head and the Heart in Culture Change

STORY 6.1 "English + Spanish + Portuguese—Building a New Culture in a Brazilian Subsidiary"
Fernando Aguirre as president at Procter & Gamble Brazil

Procter & Gamble had acquired a company called Phebo to enter into the Brazilian consumer products market. Phebo was an old and successful company in Brazil—for one thing they had a very strong position in the Brazilian soap market. P&G management had never seen anything like this, so they were reluctant to change the company they had purchased. They just said, "You guys keep doing what you've been doing," but they sent a lot of international managers (IMs) to Brazil to add more typical P&G businesses to Phebo.

The company also decided to introduce state-of-the-art technology to launch the latest and greatest products, like Pampers disposable diapers. They built a brand-new diapers factory that was managed by several international managers that cost us an arm and a leg. We had more IMs than Mexico, P&G's largest subsidiary in Latin America at the time. At one point, P&G Brazil had more than 25 IMs.

After a few years of this "benign neglect," I was asked to take over the company as the general manager. When I arrived, I found that most of the employees at the firm were from Phebo. Not surprisingly for such an old and successful company, Phebo's culture was very hierarchical in nature. People did what they were told and didn't ask many questions. Also, given the firm's market presence, most employees were pretty complacent about the company and its prospects. So most of my employees were used to being told what to do and were satisfied with the company's financial status quo.

By the way, all my employees spoke Portuguese, and only a very few could speak English. And while I spoke Spanish and English, I did not speak Portuguese. So one of my first tasks was to learn Portuguese.

Once I started digging into the numbers, it became clear that this business unit—despite its large market share in some segments—was performing very poorly. We were losing $42 million a year on an annual revenue of $80 million. For every dollar of product we sold, we lost fifty cents! When I explained our financial situation to the CEO of P&G, he couldn't believe it.

It was fairly clear to me even then that the old hierarchical and complacent culture at Phebo would not be helpful in reversing this performance. We needed change, we needed change fast, and I needed the active and creative involvement of everyone to make this change happen. We had to figure out how to survive long enough so that we could possibly grow in the future.

Of course, before I told the CEO about how bad our performance was, I had developed a three-year plan for how to turn the company around. He said it looked like a great plan but told me I had to implement it in one year, not three. And if I didn't deliver on this plan, P&G would consider exiting from Brazil.

Thus, in the beginning, I was focusing on survival, not on culture change—although it turned out that this focus on survival ended up changing the culture of the firm. One of the first actions I had to take was to choose a handful of IMs to stay and return the great majority back to other jobs. The cost of carrying an IM was in the hundreds of thousands of dollars per year per person. The decision to return most of the IMs was one of the most unpopular decisions at P&G headquarters in Cincinnati, but it was one of the most important contributors to reducing costs.

Then I started visiting the plants. The first plant I visited was in Belem, which was the main soap factory. It was the first time the company president had visited this plant in five or six years. I walked around the plant, talking to the workers. The workers saw me, heard that I was the head of the company, and were floored.

When I was in a plant, I would hold a town meeting. I would stand in front of 100, 200, or 300 employees and in my imperfect Portuguese explain what was going on. I would say, "This is our problem, and unless we turn this problem around this year, P&G is not going to stay here." They all knew that might have a big impact on them. Then I would continue, "I need ideas. Look around. Look to your left and to your right. This factory has to save $2 million. If you don't come up with ideas to do this, the people next to you may not be around because we have to fire them, or we may have to fire you, because we can't afford to keep you. I need ideas for how to save $2 million so we won't have this problem."

I said this all in my lousy Portuguese. I had a guy from HR stand next to me to correct me when I made language errors. Sometimes I had to repeat a sentence two or three times to get it right. I was told years later that the employees—most of whom were from the old hierarchical Phebo culture—were amazed by the humility I was showing: first, I came to the plant, second, I spoke in their language and was open to correction, and third, I asked for their ideas.

And we got lots of ideas from the workers. I wrote them down on a flip chart—30 or 40 potentially good ideas in each plant. These included changing the color of the soap, changing the packaging, and so forth—all from the factory workers, right there in the factory. Some were great ideas—for example, by changing the formula of the soap a little bit, we could change the packaging and save about one dollar per bar in packaging costs.

Another thing I did was change our headquarters building. My predecessor had moved the headquarters office into a beautiful office building. In order to impress the senior executives from P&G who were going to visit his operation, he had purchased beautiful artwork for the space. Each officer in the company had designed their own office and had purchased custom-made furniture. They were truly beautiful offices.

But we could not afford them. So, after reducing the size of the headquarters staff, I moved myself and my direct reports to a factory in São Paulo. I took the worst office in the factory—it backed up to the manufacturing floor and thus had no windows. Okay, there were two small windows high on one wall, but they didn't open. And instead of buying new furniture for these offices, we borrowed old furniture from the factory. At that moment, I wasn't thinking about changing the organization's culture, I was in full survival mode.

It wasn't just the offices. One of the first things my predecessor did when he arrived was to buy a new car and hire a chauffeur to drive him around. The money was in the budget for me to buy a new car, but I kept the old one. I didn't care how old it was. I had the chauffeur transferred to another role in the company.

I did a variety of other things. I and most of my top managers stopped going to so many corporate meetings. It was more important for me to stay in Brazil and work with my people to save the company than it was to travel to Cincinnati for reports and training and whatever. It also reduced our operating costs. Also, we began developing our own packaging. Cincinnati had all sorts of high-quality art and packaging skills, but they were too expensive for us. So we stopped using them.

Showing how committed I was to making the business financially sound helped when I had to negotiate some tough decisions with the union, including when I decided we needed to close a factory.

Through all these efforts, we began to turn things around. In the first year, we broke even. The second year, we made $8 million. We made $25 million in the third year, and $45 million in the fourth. Over this time period, sales went from $80 million to $450 million.

And the culture changed. The hierarchical, complacent culture of the old company—Phebo—was gone. It was replaced by a frugal, growth-oriented culture that began to deliver on the promise of Brazil for P&G.

The time came when we could afford to move our offices out of the factory. So we went back to the same offices we had left four years earlier when the company was on the brink of going out of business. However, instead of taking a whole floor, we took only half a floor. If we continued to grow the business we would increase our footprint in the building, but not before we grew the business.

We still had some of the artwork that had been purchased when we were first in that building. But I said, "No way do I want one single piece of art that hung in that building put back up. That would be like telling the people we're back to where we were four years ago."

So we never hung that art back up. We sold it or gave it away. People throughout the company heard about this decision to not hang up the artwork, and they nodded in quiet approval, because we weren't the same company we had been four years earlier.

In his efforts to build a new culture in this business unit, Fernando began by focusing on the economic reasons for changing this organization's culture—the head—and then switched his focus to building the kinds of relationships and trust with his employees needed to accomplish this change—the heart. He began with a financial analysis that showed that the business was losing money—something that appeals to the heads of employees. Then he went to the factories and, in broken Portuguese, asked the hourly employees to give him ideas about how the company could be saved—all very heart-oriented behaviors. Next, he downsized corporate headquarters and left the expensive building where this organization had been housed—very much consistent with head approaches to change. But he changed the emphasis to the heart when he moved headquarters to a factory, took the least attractive office, and filled it with leftover furniture. As the company's financial fortunes began to turn, he moved headquarters back to their original building—focusing on the head—but chose to not hang up the art that had been previously displayed at headquarters, art that he felt symbolized the old, now rejected, culture of this organization. That decision was much more about the heart of culture change.

By building stories that focused on both his employees' heads and hearts, Fernando was able to build a new lean and growth-oriented culture that has delivered high levels of financial performance for many years.

Starting with the Head in Culture Change and Then Moving to the Heart

Fernando Aguirre alternatively focused on both the head and the heart to transform his organization's culture. The public face of Marise Barroso's culture-change effort appeared to focus entirely on the heart. However, underlying the strong emotional appeal for culture change was a carefully crafted, rationally considered strategy that preceded her more emotionally oriented culture-change efforts.

> **STORY 6.2 "How Soccer Helped Us Tame a Competitive Tiger"**
> **Marise Barroso as CEO at Amanco Brazil**
>
> I knew almost as soon as I joined Amanco that we had to change the culture. Even though Amanco was the leading manufacturer and marketer of pipes and fittings for water management systems in Latin America, its operations in Brazil—even after 10 years—had bad results. We had a large and difficult competitor—Tigre Tubos e Conexões—a family-owned firm that had 60 percent of the market and a well-established brand with close to 100 percent brand recognition among customers. Tigre's advertisements focused on their quality—although our tests showed that their products were not better than ours—and how if consumers used inferior products, they would have to tear down their walls to replace the plumbing. All this enabled them to charge a 25 percent premium in the market.

After 10 long years, our employees didn't think there was much hope in improving our market position. Neither did the management team. Morale was low. But I talked to our customers. They wanted a competitor for Tigre. They were tired of having to deal with a single supplier, but they didn't see any real viable options. Our customers didn't really care who that competitor might be—and I thought, it could be us.

Our employees didn't think we could do it. I said to myself, "I've got to find a way, by using very simple and popular language, to make people—both inside the company and our customers—understand our potential. We are losing the game because we aren't even showing up to play."

Hmm. We needed to show up and play the game. And we needed to play the game in the right way. We needed to dominate the game. What game could we use as an analogy for our company to get people excited about our potential?

Of course, we were in Brazil. So it had to be soccer.

Now, I wasn't a big soccer fan. But I was operating in a very male-dominated industry, dealing with both plumbers and owners of construction material stores. I thought soccer would work with this crowd. The parallels were obvious: Amanco was about to start playing a new match. The first step was that we had to enter the field to play. If we didn't enter the field, then there was no hope. But if we entered the field, then there could be hope—and an opportunity to fight.

I took this idea to our marketing people. We decided it would take five years to completely reposition Amanco in the market. We did a careful segmentation analysis, estimated marketing costs, and so forth—all built around the theme of becoming a championship soccer team. I hired an outside advertising firm to build the ads. All of the ads—some of which later won awards—were built around becoming a championship soccer team. We took these ideas to the board, and they approved.

Moving in this direction was risky. After all, Tigre had the differentiated brand, and Amanco might be able to bring a lot of product innovation to attract customers. We could have decided to go to the low price end of the market, but we decided that we had to take on Tigre where they were—to emphasize our product quality and brand.

We had done everything we needed to do in the management team to introduce our soccer-themed marketing campaign. Now we had to take it to the world. I organized a sales convention with all our company's sales representatives, representatives from our current and potential customers, and other key stakeholders. It was the largest sales convention our company had ever put on. It was built entirely around the soccer analogy and making Amanco a championship squad.

The opening session featured Milton Neves—a soccer commentator on radio and TV, a real expert. Everyone knew him. A real soccer icon. Everyone was blown away by this first session. They were walking around saying, "What the heck is happening here?"

All the rest of the sessions in the meeting were built around soccer—how we were going to structure our attack team; what our defensive team was going to look like; how we were going to train set pieces. Soccer was a very easy way to connect to all our stakeholders. Even plumbers were drawn to the soccer analogy. The enthusiasm was contagious!

Let me give you an example of this enthusiasm in action. Our corporate color scheme was green; Tigre's was blue. I asked employees at our factories to visit some construction supply stores in their area, and cover the store in green banners, signs, balloons—anything green. We called it creating a "green wave." After covering these stores with green, our employees spontaneously started shouting "Amanco, Amanco." It became our battle cry. Pretty soon, all the salespeople had "Amanco, Amanco" as their ringtones. You heard this battle cry playing on the radio, on television. Instead of cheering for their favorite soccer team, our employees were now cheering for their company. We had "green wave" marketing campaigns all over Brazil.

We also took advantage of Tigre's weaknesses. For example, at the time, I think I was the only woman at the company's C level. For my presentation at the sales convention, I walked out on stage wearing a tiger print coat. The message was clear—we were going to fight. The sales staff went crazy! Later, we had a television commercial where a salesman wearing an Amanco T-shirt was petting a tiger's ears. Yeah, a real tiger! He made it look like it was as tame as a kitten! Our employees loved it. They loved being part of a winning team.

After all this, within just six months we went from a product with almost no brand awareness to 56 percent brand awareness. Imagine employees who used to be part of a demoralized company now realizing that Amanco was widely recognized as Tigre's major competitor. When I joined the company, Amanco had 7 percent of the market, and Tigre had 61 percent; when I left, we had 34 percent market share, and Tigre had 41 percent. I would say we not only scored a goal but were well on our way to winning the match.

The energy that Amanco's employees felt when they became convinced that they were part of a winning team was palpable. Covering a retailer with green banners and balloons, shouting "Amanco, Amanco," going crazy when they saw the boss wearing a tiger print jacket on stage—all these suggest that Marise was very successful in addressing the hearts of her employees in changing Amanco's culture. When employees at Amanco began to believe they were part of a winning team, they began acting like it. And when their customers became convinced that Amanco was a winning team, they also began acting like it.

However, all this emphasis on the heart of culture change at Amanco was preceded by very careful and systematic financial and strategic analyses, including a careful segmentation analysis of the market, a thoughtfully planned marketing campaign, and difficult strategic choices (e.g., to go after a differentiated market segment that already had a tough competitor). All of this rational economic work was done behind the scenes but provided a rigorous economic basis for engaging in the culture change Marise was planning. In this case, the head part of culture change was used to provide a rationale for the heart part of this change.

Without appealing to the head, the emotional outbursts and enthusiasm created by Marise's soccer analogy in soccer-crazy Brazil may not have added up to any real change—just an exciting sales meeting that didn't enable Amanco to really compete against Tigre. Marise's team had a plan to follow up on this enthusiasm, to turn it into market share. On the other hand, without appealing to the heart, Marise's analysis of the market and strategy would be—frankly—boring. It was the enthusiasm of her employees that made the implications of these formal analyses real.

Starting with the Heart of Cultural Change to Get to the Head of This Change

Scott Robinson, a young manager given the apparently impossible task of mending union relations in a factory, took exactly the opposite approach to Marise Barroso. Where Marise did the rational analysis first and then focused on the emotions to change the culture at Amanco, Scott focused on the heart of culture change first and then moved to the rational economics of negotiating with the union.

STORY 6.3 "Changing the Culture with the Union"
Scott Robinson as human resources manager at Federal
Signal Corporation

I was 23 years old when I was asked to negotiate a new contract with the union.

To say we had a union problem at the plant was an understatement. They didn't like us, and we didn't like them. At the time I was given this assignment, there were 110 outstanding grievances. Historically, it had taken months to get a three-year agreement, and even when we came to an agreement, there was deep animosity between the company and the union. Whenever the union could do something to hurt the company, they did. And whenever management could do something to screw the union, they did. For more than 20 years, the company and the union developed this dislike for each other. They took all this personally and tried to make each other's lives as miserable as possible.

I thought this was silly. The plant needed its 1,600 union employees to get the work done, and these 1,600 employees needed the jobs in the plant. So I took a different approach.

Before negotiations started, I asked the company president if I could meet with the union leader. He agreed, so the union leader—his name was John— and I met together at an informal lunch. It was supposed to be a one-hour meeting, but four and a half hours later, we had come to a common understanding that the current state of union relations in the plant was just silly, it was our job to fix this relationship, and we could do it if we really wanted to.

So, with my staff, I did the homework. We looked for ways we could adjust the current contract to save money and how we could use these cost savings to pay the union more. Long story short, we negotiated a new contract in three weeks—not several months—we got rid of all 110 grievances, saved the company about $6 million in costs, and used these savings to give the union more money per hour than they originally asked for.

This began creating a whole new culture in the plant, a culture where management and the union could work together. Of course, it took time for certain union employees and certain managers to get used to this new culture, but the change began when the union leader, John, and I decided that we could do things differently, that we could solve the historical animosity between the union and management.

Scott started by building a relationship with the union leader. That initial lunch meeting was not a first negotiating session. Its purpose was to discover if Scott and the union leader, John, could find common ground. Could they trust each other enough so that, together, they could create a new way of managing firm/union negotiations? Could they work together to change the entire employee culture at the firm?

Building a trusting relationship with the union leader first—working on the heart of culture change—made it possible later on to find ways to help both the company and the union succeed. The company succeeded by getting more flexible work rules that reduced their costs; the union succeeded by appropriating some of these reduced costs for their members. All of this was driven by the economic agreements that were made between the union and the firm, agreements that depended, in the first place, on having a trusting relationship between the two leaders of this negotiation.

Imagine the surprise of the union negotiators when Scott offered a higher wage increase than the union had asked for, a wage increase made possible by cost efficiencies created through a more cooperative relationship between the union and the firm. Indeed, sometimes cultural change starts with the heart but very much, in the end, relies on the rational analyses of the head.

Integrating the Head and the Heart of Cultural Change

Whether you alternate between appealing to the heart and head of culture change, start with an emphasis on the head and then move to the heart, or start with a focus on the heart and then move to the head, one thing is clear: Successful culture change requires both an appeal to the rational economic interests of your employees—their heads—and to their emotional and social interests—their hearts. Do the first (head) without the second (heart), and it is difficult to build the personal enthusiasm and commitment necessary for culture change. Do the second without the first, and it is difficult to realize the economic benefits of culture change.

One firm in our sample that seems to integrate these two dimensions of culture change very effectively is DaVita. Note how, in this story, Mike Staffieri built stories that exemplified the culture that DaVita was trying to implement, and how these stories appealed to their employees' heads and hearts.

STORY 6.4 "Making Our Commitments Real"
Mike Staffieri as COO at DaVita

As a health care company in the kidney dialysis business, we try to organize around something we call the "Trilogy of Care": caring for patients, caring for each other, and caring for the world. We think these three forms of caring are tightly connected and form the basis of a sustainable business model. But just having these slogans pasted on some banner or painted on the wall doesn't mean anything. We needed to find ways to make this idea real.

We decided to start talking about DaVita as a village. People work and live in their village. And people in a village care for each other. To help make this idea real, we created what we call Village Programs. These are very specific programs and activities that reinforce that we are a community first and a company second.

An example of a Village Program is the DaVita Village Network. This program pools contributions from the company and the donations of employees to provide support for those who are experiencing a hardship. Our employees can make payroll contributions to this network, or they can make one-time contributions. And if any one of our employees—we call them teammates—runs into difficult times, they can apply for grants from the network to help them out. For example, if somebody's child has cancer, and they can't work, and they've got health bills piling up, they can apply for a grant. In addition, their local teams will often do some simple fundraising—like a bake sale or something like that—to help out. And then they apply to the DaVita Village Network, which sometimes matches up to 10 times (or more) the funds that are raised locally.

A good example of the DaVita Village Network is what happened when Hurricane Harvey hit Houston. As you may remember, that was a total disaster, with terrible flooding and lots of people losing their homes. We had 110 clinics in Houston. Our people were amazing. Their homes were flooded, they had nowhere to go, and they still came into work because if they didn't, their patients could get really sick and have to go into the hospital. Sometimes our patients die when they don't get their treatments. And so, while some of our employees had nothing, they were still committed to their patients—"Caring for patients" is the first part of our Trilogy of Care.

I flew down to Houston with a group of senior leaders. We flew as close as we could to Houston and then drove down the rest of the way. We brought $75,000 in cash with us from the Village Network. We went around all our clinics and met with our employees to find out who had the most immediate financial needs—like renting a hotel room or eating out at restaurants. Employees in this situation automatically got $800 from the DaVita Village Network—no hassles, no paperwork.

We also flew down lots of volunteers from corporate headquarters to Houston. They went to our team members' homes to rip out ruined carpet or tear out drywall. This is what our team members would have been doing, but they had to go to the clinics to care for their patients. "Caring for each other" is the second part of our Trilogy of Care.

The DaVita Village Network did all this—put our team members up in hotels, bought them toiletry kits, gave them money for food. I know that slogans like "Caring for patients, caring for each other, and caring for the world" can ring hollow in some companies. But Hurricane Harvey showed me that the DaVita Village is real. It showed me that sometimes the best way we can take care of our patients is to take care of each other.

We use this same approach in "caring for the world." In most developed countries, either private insurance or governments pay for dialysis. This is not the case in many developing countries. In these countries, people can die because they do not have access to treatment. We help set up and support medical missions around the globe to fund dialysis clinics. In this way, we try to complete our commitment to the Trilogy of Care.

Look, I believe in the idea that our company is a community, that DaVita is like a village where we take care of each other. Let me give you an example of what this means. The wife of a good friend of mine was going through breast cancer. They lived in Florida, but they were going to Memorial Sloan Kettering Cancer Center in New York to get her treatment. At the time, my office was in California, but I happened to be in Chicago the day before her surgery. I decided to stay in the East a little longer, and I went to New York and surprised my friend at the surgery center on the day his wife was in surgery. I knew he'd just be sitting there in a waiting room, scared to death about what was happening with his wife, miles from home, not knowing anyone. So I went and sat with him during his wife's surgery. I think it meant a lot to him.

I didn't tell anyone that I had done this. Only my assistant knew, because he had made the air reservations. But he told everyone. I don't like telling these stories about myself, but they get out. When people tell these stories, it paints their leader in a different light. It says, "Yeah, Mike is a tough guy, and he's really all about performance. But he also has this human side." For me, my team, my direct reports, are like my family. I had no idea that this friend of mine would tell this story in front of a meeting of almost 5,000 people.

Another example. Two weeks ago, I flew out to Cincinnati because I have a direct report who just had a baby and is out on maternity leave for four months. And I thought, how great would it be if your boss showed up and came and met the baby—flew across the country and spent a half day with you just to show you that he's been thinking about you while you are out. Yeah, that stuff takes a lot of time, and it's hard to assign a value to it, but when you have people that you love and that are great and that you know are highly valuable and being recruited all the time, showing them that you care is a big deal.

I don't talk about these episodes very much, but they get out.

DaVita's business model—"Care for patients, care for each other, care for the world" sounds idealistic and unreal. A bit dreamy. Like it is all heart and no head. And yet, by taking care of each other, DaVita employees are able to more effectively take care of their patients—even in extreme settings like the flooding in Houston. And by taking care of their patients, DaVita ensures its long-term financial viability—very much a head-oriented justification for culture change.

Conclusion

Thus, our research suggests that culture change must appeal both to the head—the economic reasons for engaging in such change—and the heart—the emotional and social reasons to engage in such change. Head-only culture-change efforts fail because they do not incorporate the deeply social nature of organizational cultures. Heart-only culture-change efforts fail because they do not incorporate the fundamental economic purpose of most kinds of organizations.

One historical figure who understood better than most both the head and the heart of organizational change was Abraham Lincoln. One of the great storytellers in US history, Lincoln drew on his experiences as an itinerant lawyer in the rural West to build stories to emotionally connect with his constituents and colleagues.[1] Often humorous and sometimes racy, Lincoln's stories invariably made fundamental points about critical issues of his day, including the issue of slavery. But Lincoln did not rely just on the "heart" of his stories to enable change. He also focused on the "head" of organizational change. This balance between head and heart can be seen very clearly in Lincoln's efforts to get the Thirteenth Amendment—which constitutionally banned slavery—passed by the US House of Representatives.[2]

The year 1865 was critical for President Abraham Lincoln. The Civil War between the Union and Confederate states continued past its fourth year. The cataclysm of carnage unleashed by that war was unprecedented. Ultimately, over 640,000 people died in the Civil War—nearly 1 out of every 30 US citizens at the time. And while the war seemed to be grinding to a close toward the end of 1864, there would still be much blood shed before Lee surrendered to Grant at Appomattox Court House on April 9, 1865.

Politically, Lincoln had been reelected to the presidency in a landslide over his former chief general, George McClellan. His political party—the Republican Party—also increased its majority in the Senate and House of Representatives. This meant that there were 20 or so Democrats who had not been reelected to the House who would be out of a job once the new Congress was convened in March 1865.

Lincoln saw an opportunity here. He originally signed the Emancipation Proclamation on January 1, 1863. However, this proclamation only freed the slaves in those states that, at the time, were in rebellion against the United States. Lincoln had signed the Emancipation Proclamation as a military necessity, but its enforceability after the war was uncertain. He was convinced that the only way to fully do away with the institution of slavery was to amend the US Constitution—a process that would begin with two-thirds of the Senate and House of Representatives voting in favor of a proposed constitutional amendment.

Indeed, the Senate had already voted in favor of the amendment. Only the House vote remained before the antislavery amendment—the Thirteenth Amendment to the US Constitution—could be sent out to states for final ratification. However, passage in the House was less certain.

The possible end of the war also created in Lincoln an urgency to get a positive vote on this amendment. If the war ended, and the former Confederate States of America were readmitted to the Union with their former rights and status, this could make it more difficult to get the amendment through the US legislative system. Also, Lincoln wanted bipartisan support for the Thirteenth Amendment and so wanted it ratified before the new Congress was convened in March 1865.

Lincoln used two kinds of arguments to support the ratification of the Thirteenth Amendment. The first focused on the heart—slavery was immoral and by all rights should already have been abolished in the United States. By 1864, the horrors of slavery were well known and the debate among Republicans had shifted from whether or not slavery should be outlawed to how it should be outlawed. Lincoln's moral arguments for abolishing slavery are powerful, even more than a century and a half later:

> The abolition of slavery by constitutional provision settles the fate, for all coming time, not only of the millions now in bondage, but of unborn millions to come.[3]

However, the official line of the Democratic Party in 1864 was that bringing an end to the Civil War was more important than outlawing slavery and that, in fact, preemptively outlawing slavery might prolong rather than shorten the war. Thus, while the Republicans had a majority of the seats in the House, they did not have the two-thirds majority required to pass a constitutional amendment on to the states. In this setting, the 20 or so "lame duck" Democrats who would be out of government with the new Congress were individuals whom Lincoln believed could be persuaded—if not by an appeal to their hearts, perhaps with an appeal to their heads—to vote for the amendment.

The president then, and still today, appoints people to many government jobs. It is not uncommon for the president to use these patronage appointments to reward loyalty or other service to the government. Lincoln decided to use these appointments as an inducement for those leaving government service to vote in favor of the Thirteenth Amendment, especially not-reelected Democrats who had previously voted against the amendment. While not getting directly involved in providing these inducements

to these soon-to-be-unemployed government officials, Lincoln made his interest in this matter clear when instructing those given this responsibility:

> I leave it to you to determine how it shall be done; but remember I am pres-
> ident of the United States, clothed with immense power, and I expect you
> to procure the votes.[4]

Clearly, Lincoln had concluded that if it wasn't possible to get these soon-
to-be-unemployed congressmen to vote for the Thirteenth Amendment
because it was the morally right thing to do, perhaps he could get them to
change their vote so that they could enhance their future employment opportunities. A variety of plum government appointments went to Democrats leaving the House. In most cases, those Democrats voted for the
Thirteenth Amendment.

As bells throughout Washington, D.C., rang in celebration, the Thirteenth Amendment to the US Constitution was passed by the House of
Representatives on January 31, 1865, by a final vote of 119–56, four votes
more than the required two-thirds majority. The Civil War ended on April 9,
1865, when General Lee surrendered the Army of Northern Virginia to
General Grant at the Appomattox Court House in Virginia. And the Thirteenth Amendment was finally ratified by the states on December 6, 1865.

Tragically, Lincoln would not live to see the legal abolition of slavery. He
was shot by John Wilkes Booth on April 14, 1865, and died the next morning, just six days after Lee's surrender. But Lincoln's ability to appeal both
to the heart and to the head of members of the House of Representatives
ensured the passage and subsequent ratification of the Thirteenth Amendment and the abolition of legal slavery in the United States—a profound cultural change that has rung true for over a century and a half.

Are you willing to appeal to both the heads and the hearts of your employees in your effort to change your organization's culture?

CHAPTER SEVEN

Story Building as Theater

The three of us have all had deep experience in helping organizations change their cultures—both as senior executives and as consultants. This experience meant that most of the elements of successful culture-changing stories we identified from our research did not completely surprise us. Certainly, before we collected our database of stories, we had not systematically done the analysis to identify these attributes. But after we generated this list from the analysis of our database, it had a face validity that was consistent with our prior experience.

Except for the attribute of successful culture-changing stories discussed in this chapter: theater. Of course, each of us had seen CEOs engage in some pretty theatrical behaviors to drive home some point about the culture they wanted to create in their organizations. What was surprising, however, was how widespread this theatricality was in our database.

What Is Theater in the Context of Cultural Change?

What do we mean by theatrical? Like so many aspects of building stories, what is theatrical is much easier to see than it is to define. Generally, it involves top leaders in a firm doing something very different from their normal day-to-day activities, doing this in a very public setting, and doing it in a way that reinforces some aspect of a cultural change that this leader is trying to implement. Surprisingly, it often also involves this leader dressing up in a costume, taking on a role that is very different from who they really are, and generally acting in a very strange way. Thus, the label: Theater.

Roughly half the successful culture-change stories in our database had some elements of theater. Thus, unlike the other attributes of successful culture-change stories identified from the analysis of our story database, theater does not seem to be a necessary condition for building a story that actually changes a culture. However, it is common enough, and its effects can be sufficiently dramatic—pun intended—that it is worth mentioning. Think of theater as another tool in your tool kit for building a culture-changing story. You may not have to use this tool very often, but it's nice to have in your inventory.

Why Theater?

Adding an element of theater to building a culture-changing story has several advantages. For one thing, theatrical elements make the story memorable. In our experience, employees can remember theatrical elements of a story for many years—sometimes long after how the theater fit in with a culture-changing story is forgotten.

They also signify a leader's willingness to do whatever is necessary to implement a new culture—even if these actions might be somewhat embarrassing and way out of character. But in some sense, that is the point of these theatrical elements—because they are somewhat embarrassing and way out of character, theatrical elements demonstrate a leader's commitment to culture change. It is yet another example of leaders planting a stake in the ground to help change their organization's culture.

Finally, the theatrical elements of the culture-changing stories are fun. Fun for the leader, fun for the employees. To many, culture change sounds like endless meetings with change management specialists, generating lists of core values, developing long and boring training meetings, and so forth. Culture change, in this world, is a long, dark tunnel out of which a firm never really emerges.

But theater is fun. It's a bit crazy. It's out of the ordinary. And, to the extent that it reinforces cultural change, it can help enable that change in tangible and real ways. Our first example of using theater to help facilitate culture change takes place at a company that was not having fun—indeed, it was meeting to finalize a large layoff. But what occurred at this meeting was very theatrical and started this company back on the path toward financial success.

A Different Kind of Celebratory Dinner

> **STORY 7.1 "A Bread and Water Celebration"**
> **Jeff Rodek as CEO at Hyperion Solutions**
>
> I joined the board of Arbor Software as an independent director in early 1998. During my discussions with the board and the CEO prior to joining, I was told that a merger had been considered but was now no longer being considered. However, at my first board meeting it was back on the table for a vote and was approved. The Arbor/Hyperion merger turned out to be an initial disaster and about a year later I was recruited and hired to be chairman and CEO. In my first nine months with the new Hyperion, we were enjoying pretty good levels of success. We thought we were pretty talented, but we were losing key staff to other technology companies who were offering large equity incentives to our management. We thought we had a somewhat clear strategy post-merger and a reasonably strong culture, but as I was soon to learn, a degree of self-satisfaction and complacency permeated the organization, along with a strategy that needed to be much clearer.
>
> In retrospect, probably what was really happening during those first nine months was that the entire software segment in the economy was doing well, and—after identifying some early easy wins—we were doing well right along with the industry. We weren't nearly as good as we thought we were and as our historical performance suggested we could be.
>
> Of course, all of that changed when there was a downturn in the industry. Our key sales account executives and leaders were leaving, and the weaknesses of our operational processes became apparent. We were not performing up to expectations, and worse, we were losing money and burning cash. This led to a large revenue and earnings miss in the fourth quarter of my first year. We righted the ship modestly, but the board and I felt we were just muddling along.
>
> We engaged an outside consulting firm and developed a clearer strategy that necessitated a layoff. To finalize the resulting plan and achieve buy-in, we scheduled an offsite meeting for the executive team and about a dozen other key staff. When I looked at the calendar and saw that we had booked a fancy dining room and ballroom in an expensive hotel in San Francisco—the Fairmont—for this meeting, I was shocked. There was no

way we could be seen as celebrating such bad performance in this fancy hotel.

I called my executive assistant and the meeting planner into my office and told them that we would have to cancel the venue. My assistant's face dropped—"We've already paid for the venue. Because of the technology industry downturn, we got an extremely low rate. We can cancel, but we will be on the hook for the whole thing whether we use the hotel or not."

Well, that didn't sound like a good idea. However, even with a low rate, the appearance of holding a meeting at the Fairmont Hotel—with its ornate dining room and breathtaking views—was just not acceptable, to me or any employee who heard about this meeting. So, I decided to change the event a bit—without my senior team knowing about it.

On the appointed day, at the appointed time, people began coming into the dining room for our kickoff dinner. The table was set beautifully— sparkling silverware and crystal goblets surrounding exquisite china. Just what you would expect at a hotel like this one. Expectations for an excellent dinner were high.

And then the waiters began serving dinner. They poured tap water and served bread. I stood to address the team with my pre-dinner comments, but first I began by playing Elton John's "Funeral for a Friend." As the music progressed, I explained, "Normally, I would have canceled this event. It's not just the cost, it's the appearance—and we don't have the right to celebrate our dismal performance. We all know it's been terrible. We have let down our customers, employees, and shareholders. So I have decided to serve the only menu that we, as a company, deserve tonight. Bread and water. That is all we will get tonight, that is all we deserve tonight. Bread and water."

There were quiet nods of agreement throughout the room.

I also stated that if anyone so much as expensed a Snickers bar that evening, they would be terminated.

I will say that the bread served by the hotel was excellent!

I continued, "My expectation is that we will solve the problems we are facing this year, and that next year we will completely turn the performance of the firm around. I want to be back in this ballroom next year. In fact, I want to schedule a celebration dinner in this very room one year from today. But I don't want to serve bread and water next year. I want to have an opulent meal. I want us all to deserve an opulent meal."

In many ways, the company's turnaround began that night—with a meal of bread and water. And the following year, as we celebrated our success, we all remembered where we had been the year before, and committed to never having a bread and water dinner again.

Jeff Rodek used a supposed celebratory dinner as an unfreezing event to get his organization ready for the cultural change they would need to turn its performance around.[1] That required transforming a complacent, self-satisfied culture into a lean and hungry culture—a perfect analogy for a "bread and water" dinner.

Jeff turned this dinner into a theatrical event in a couple of ways. First, he made the changes to the menu himself, without informing any of his senior team. Second, he kept the changes secret. Third, when his team came into the venue, it appeared that it was going to be yet another typical celebratory dinner—with fancy plates, silverware, and food.

In short, he set them up perfectly.

One can imagine the confusion as the initial bread course was followed by a second bread course, and then a third. And no wine—just still and sparkling water.

With the impeccable timing of a professional comedian, Jeff then stood up and revealed the punchline: Tonight, we only deserve bread and water.

We are quite sure that every employee who attended that dinner remembers this message. And they remember how this began a process of changing a self-satisfied and complacent culture into an aggressive and growth-oriented culture. As important, a year later they had a real celebratory dinner.

Breaking Down the Academic Hierarchy

As the first female dean of the Marriott School of Business at Brigham Young University, Brigitte Madrian had two cultural challenges to overcome in order to develop a closer connection to her students: expectations about her "proper role" as a woman, and expectations about her "proper role" as a dean. She chose to use theater to begin to address these issues.

STORY 7.2 **"Using a Harry Potter Theme to Reduce Student Fears"**
Brigitte Madrian as dean of the Marriott School of Business

Universities are very formal organizations, especially around senior administrative offices like presidents and deans. Students sometimes feel very uncomfortable being around administrators—and sometimes, administrators feel uncomfortable being around the students. There is often a cultural gap between the administration and our students.

That gap was even wider for me, because I was the first woman dean in our school. So, not only did students not know how to act around a dean, they really didn't know how to act around a woman dean.

I wanted to try to break this gap down. I wanted our school to be rigorous and demanding, yes, but not intimidating and scary. I wanted the students to be comfortable. I was convinced that if they are more comfortable in their surroundings, they will be more successful in their classes, and that this is good for the students, for faculty, for the companies that hire our students—in short, for just about everyone.

And I wanted to have some fun.

I started with some simple things—a "Deans and Doughnuts" program, where my associate deans and I passed out doughnuts to students walking through our building. I started attending the meetings of various student groups and clubs, just so the students would get used to being around me. These were helpful and began to change the culture, but I wanted to do more.

I love the Harry Potter movies, and Halloween was just three weeks away. I decided to dress up like one of the characters in the Harry Potter movies, Dolores Umbridge, and use that as an opportunity to interact with the students.

Dolores Umbridge is the evil headmistress who comes into the Hogwarts school, displaces one of the great heroes of the series—the headmaster Dumbledore—and starts issuing hundreds of "educational edicts" that actually have little or nothing to do with enhancing education. These edicts were plastered on a wall for all the students to read.

In addition, if any student did anything out of line—or really, anything that Dolores didn't like—that student was assigned detention. Late for class—detention; hair not combed—detention; surly attitude—detention.

My guess was that some of our students thought that being the dean of a business school was like being Dolores Umbridge, that my job was to walk around making sure that faculty and students did what they were supposed to do, and if they didn't, to correct them. I wanted to disabuse them of this belief by playing the role of Dolores Umbridge from Harry Potter and having fun with it.

I bought a pink dress—Dolores always dressed in pink. Dolores liked cats, so I bought a stuffed cat, and a cute pink purse. I had our facilities people play Dolores's theme song on a loop in our building, and our communications staff developed dozens of "educational edicts" that we plastered on the walls of our building. Some of my associate deans also dressed up as characters from Harry Potter. We walked around the building, and I would go up to a student and say, "Hmm, late for class—detention." Then I would give them a piece of candy. Or "Shirt untucked—detention," or "Shoe untied—detention," all followed by a piece of candy.

This was a generation of students raised on Harry Potter, so everyone instantly got the joke. Of course, it was fun. Of course, the students talked about it for days. But it also sent a message—I may be the dean of the school, and I may be the first woman dean of the school, but you don't have to be afraid of me. We are in this educational business together, and the best way we can succeed is to work together as effectively as possible.

And, along the way, maybe we can have some fun.

This is a great use of theater to begin to break down cultural barriers that could otherwise interfere with the educational mission of the school. Of course, by itself, this event would be unlikely to set aside a hierarchical academic culture that has existed for literally centuries. But it was a beginning.

Can a Pair of Shorts Really Change an Organization's Culture?

STORY 7.3 "My Fashion Statement"
Shane Kim as CEO at GameStop

I came to GameStop as the CEO after several years at Microsoft. At Microsoft, people wore what they wanted to wear to work, unless you were going to meet a customer. Well, GameStop headquarters was in Dallas, Texas, and the morning I arrived, it was already over 100 degrees. But when I looked around, no one was wearing shorts. Turns out that GameStop had a policy against wearing shorts to work.

GameStop was going through a difficult time. People were worried about the future. Many senior managers at the company had left, there were challenges presented by increasing disintermediation in the console gaming market, and growing interest in the company by private equity firms. I wanted to loosen things up so that people could relax and have fun at work. Letting people wear shorts to work was a small thing, but it could help.

We decided to announce the new shorts policy by making a funny video. The video began by showing me talking in some meetings, writing on the whiteboard, and so forth. The video showed only the top half of my body, and I was dressed in a dark suit and tie. Then, toward the end of the video, the shot changed to a full body view of me and showed me wearing shorts and long black socks with black shoes with my suit coat and tie—which is a very bad look, by the way. I looked directly into the camera and said, "From now on, it's okay to wear shorts to the office."

The reaction to this video was amazing. It was like I had put a chicken into every pot. It wasn't just that we could wear shorts to work. It was also about the fact that we could have fun at work. This move was so popular that we were able to begin to address some of the more fundamental challenges facing the company.

This story was actually on video, so it was intentionally theatrical in nature. And funny. But remember, this story wasn't just about wearing shorts to work, it was about engaging employees in a way that would help them relax and have fun at work, while at the same time addressing the difficult challenges facing the firm.

Developing a More Creative Culture

STORY 7.4 "My Steven Tyler Impersonation"
Greg Tunney as CEO at RG Barry Corporation

I had already been CEO of RG Barry Corporation for several years. RG Barry operated in a variety of "functional fashion" businesses—including slippers (under the Dearfoams brand) and travel bags (under the Baggallini brand). Competing in these businesses required an innovative and creative culture—even though our products were highly functional in nature, they also had to have a fashionable flare.

The founder of RG Barry had been chair of the board for many years. While a skilled merchandiser, he had created a pretty conservative and cautious culture. That culture sometimes got in the way of us pursuing new and innovative business activities, and new and interesting fashions. I felt like we had to break out of this tradition if the company was going to progress like I wanted.

I decided to use our annual retreat as a place to begin this transformation. Working with an outside consultant, we had our management team divide up into three groups. Each group was asked to develop and present a funny skit about the company and its culture. There were to be three judges—the consultant, our corporate HR manager, and me, the CEO.

This was all consistent with the *American Idol* format that was popular on TV at the time. Three recent judges on *American Idol* had been Simon Cowell, Jennifer Lopez, and Steven Tyler. Steven Tyler was the lead singer of Aerosmith—and looked every bit the part of the lead singer in a rock band.

So, to parallel the *American Idol* show, it was decided that the consultant would dress up like Simon Cowell, our corporate HR manager would dress up like Jennifer Lopez, and I would dress up like Steven Tyler.

Steven Tyler was, to say the least, the most flamboyant judge on *American Idol*. Ever. To dress up like him, I wore skin-tight leopard-skin pants, a loose fitting partially ripped shirt, several colorful scarves, topped off with a long black wig. After "Steven Tyler" was announced as the third judge, I came running into the room where the skits were going to be presented. My team went crazy. They laughed and cheered—I think they could not have imagined that the CEO of the company would dress up that way.

Truthfully, I looked ridiculous. But to me, it was about introducing a less formal, more fun, more creative culture into the company. Over the years, no one remembered which skit won the *American Idol* contest. They did, however, remember that the CEO once dressed up as Steven Tyler— which gave some of our people the courage to begin to think outside the box about functional fashion.

A CEO dressing up as Steven Tyler is very theatrical. But it also sent a memorable message—let's have fun, let's be creative, let's use that creativity to ramp up our functional fashion businesses. Interestingly, Brigitte Madrian and Greg Tunney were not the only leaders in our story database to dress up like someone else to make a point about how their organizational culture needed to change.

One leader of a Chinese subsidiary of an international firm we know wanted to drive home to his employees how important it was for them to learn about and respect Chinese culture. To make this point, he dressed up as the Chinese philosopher Sun Tzu and passed out copies of Sun Tzu's famous book *The Art of War* to all the managers who attended their division-wide management meeting. Then, still in costume, this leader presented his division's new strategy using the structure and format that were in Sun Tzu's book. In other management meetings, he dressed up as other famous figures in Chinese history, including Chairman Mao.

Some people might see business leaders dressing up as famous characters in Chinese history as inappropriate cultural misappropriation. But the people at this firm didn't see it this way—after all, this leader was not pretending that he was becoming a famous Chinese philosopher or political leader. Instead, they saw it for what it was—honoring the Chinese culture, emphasizing its impact and importance for the company. Developing this respect for Chinese culture was an essential element in this organization's success in China.

And it was fun.

Announcing Quarterly Results

Nothing is quite as boring as announcing quarterly financial results. These meetings sometimes even put accountants to sleep. One leader in our sample decided to use changes in these painful meetings as a way to further reduce the formal and hierarchical culture at the organization where he worked.

STORY 7.5 "Dressing Up to Deliver the Financial Results"
The CEO of a global corporation

When I arrived at the company as the CEO, the firm had a very formal and hierarchical organizational culture. The CEO in this firm was almost deified.

It didn't take much to figure out that I probably wasn't going to hear the truth about problems in the company if employees thought that I was unapproachable or aloof. So I decided to shake things up.

One way I did this was to wear a costume when I announced our quarterly results. I would dress up in crazy ways—as a pop music singer, as a dinosaur, or as a wild animal—to share the results.

The people in these meetings went crazy when they saw me dress up in costumes. It was just a little way of making people detach from this idea of the deification of the CEO, that kind of image of the CEO being like the pope or something. In this way, people could see the CEO simply as a human being and listen with goodwill to what I had to say.

Reaffirming an Organization's Changed Culture

Firms that have successfully changed their cultures can use theatrical management to reaffirm and celebrate that change. Consider the use of theater at DaVita.

Story 7.6 "All for One, and One for All"
Mike Staffieri as COO at DaVita

We wanted to find ways to celebrate our culture of being a village and being there for each other. It turned out that some of the senior team really liked the teamwork and imagery of the Three Musketeers. There is this scene in one of the Three Musketeers movies where the king tells a new generation of Musketeers to kill the current Musketeers. In response, the current Musketeers raise their swords and put them together and shout, "If we must die, let it be like this! All for one, and one for all!"

Well, we got a hold of this film, and we changed the dialogue on the film to "If we must dialyze, let us dialyze like this! All for one, and one for all!"

We adopted the "All for one, and one for all!" message that we still use today to close out our live events, calls, and teammate messages to reinforce the sentiment that we're all in this together.

For a long time, we showed this version of the film at training meetings as part of our onboarding process. Many of our frontline workers, including dieticians, social workers, nurses, and patient care technicians, have seen this film clip. We have also built a complete "dialysis" version of the Three Musketeers story that goes with the clip.

In fact, whenever there was a graduation from some kind of training, the people leading the graduation—senior managers like myself—dressed up in Three Musketeers outfits as we officiated at the graduation. There will typically be anywhere from 500 to 1,000 people in the audience at these graduations, and we would show the revised film clip, talk about what it means to DaVita, and then after the ceremony, people could come up to the stage with their families and have their pictures taken with one or more of the Three Musketeers!

It's fun, but it also sends a message of the kind of company we are and that we want to be.

Obviously, the range of theatricality we saw in our culture-change story database was very broad. Some CEOs were very theatrical—staging memorable events, dressing up like famous characters, and so forth. Others were less so—although even relatively less theatrical culture-change stories nevertheless often had some theatrical elements in them. For example, in Story 1.1, where Manoel Amorim invited the call center worker to make a presentation to the executive committee of the company—that was pretty theatrical.

However, we understand that not all business leaders will be comfortable with the theatricality that is sometimes used to build and reinforce their culture-changing stories. That is probably why we see such theatricality in only about half of the culture-changing stories in our database. But for those who are comfortable with theatricality, it can be very helpful in building, reinforcing, and helping people remember these stories. And all this increases the probability that the stories built by these leaders will actually create cultural change.

Conclusion

Theatricality has played an important role in many of the historical examples of culture change described in this book. Gandhi—with his famous walk to the sea described in Chapter 4—was a master of the theatrical elements of social movements. When Nelson Mandela wore a Springboks shirt at the Rugby World Cup final in South Africa—described in Chapter 5—

he was engaging in theater. And when Abraham Lincoln would spin one of his folksy backwoods tales to help convince a member of the House of Representatives to vote for the Thirteenth Amendment—as described in Chapter 6—he was engaging in a very personal form of theater. But theater also played a surprisingly important role in abolishing the slave trade in the United Kingdom.

The effort to ban the slave trade in the United Kingdom was an early example of what is now called a social movement.[2] These movements often incorporate many theatrical elements, and this was certainly the case with efforts to ban the slave trade.[3] Political leaders of this effort would host parties for their colleagues that included former slaves who would share their stories with the other guests. Rallies and demonstrations demanding an end to the slave trade and supporting efforts consistent with this goal—like not eating sugar produced by slaves in the Caribbean—were commonplace. Multiple 50-foot-long petitions, each containing thousands of signatures calling for the end of the slave trade, were flamboyantly unrolled on the floor of the House of Commons.

But the first successful vote against the slave trade in the House of Commons required a different kind of theater—the proponents of anti-slave trade legislation pretending that nothing was afoot as their legislation went forward.

The leader of the anti–slave trade movement in the British House of Commons was William Wilberforce. Born in 1759, the son and grandson of wealthy merchants, Wilberforce was independently wealthy by his early 20s. While still a student at St. John's College, Cambridge, he was elected to Parliament. However, he did not become a force in the anti–slave trade movement until several years later, after his religious conversion to evangelical Christianity in 1784.

The slave trade existed between Great Britain, the west coast of Africa, and the New World—North and South America, including the Caribbean. Trade goods were shipped from ports in Great Britain to West Africa where they were sold. These revenues were then used to purchase human beings from the interior of the continent, who were then shipped to the New World, where these people were sold into slavery. The results of slave labor in the New World—cotton, sugar, and rum—were then exported back to Great Britain.

At its height, the slave trade generated about 80 percent of Great Britain's foreign income. British ships, flying various national flags, carried 40,000 enslaved people per year from Africa to the New World through the notorious Middle Passage. On average, 20 percent of the enslaved transported on these ships died while at sea.

The first petition to eliminate the slave trade was sent to the British House of Commons in 1783. It was ignored. The first bill to abolish the slave trade was voted on in the House of Commons in April 1791. It lost 163 to 88. Another bill was introduced a year later, in April 1792. It lost 230 to 85. A third bill was introduced in February 1793. It lost by 8 votes. This pattern was repeated many times over the years.

During this period, the supporters of the abolition of the slave trade continued to hold rallies, pass around petitions, write books, and give speeches. Despite all these efforts, the movement had little success.

Then Wilberforce and his colleagues developed a new plan. Instead of making the introduction of the abolition of the slave trade a large theatrical event, they had a colleague—not a particularly strong supporter of banning the slave trade—introduce a "small" bill called the Foreign Slave Trade Abolition Bill in the House of Commons. This bill, introduced when the House was largely empty, simply banned British subjects from aiding or abetting slave trading with any of the French colonies. Since at the time Britain was at war with France, such a ban was hardly seen as controversial. In fact, it was fully consistent with preventing the French from efficiently engaging in their war efforts.

However, since many British ships—often under the American flag—were engaging in this trade, banning the slave trade with French colonies was, indirectly, banning the slave trade altogether. The bill passed in the House of Commons and received Royal Assent on May 23, 1806.

Theater played two roles in the passage of this act. First, the supporters of banning the slave trade had to act as if the Foreign Slave Trade Abolition Bill had little or nothing to do with the slave trade per se—a clever piece of acting for people so passionately committed to this cause. Second, why was the House of Commons so empty on the day when this bill was proposed? Turns out that Wilberforce had invited, and paid for, the entire House of Commons to attend a theatrical event that afternoon. Those who opposed banning the slave trade could not vote against this "small" bill because they were being entertained at the theater.

The following year, a bill that banned the slave trade outright was passed. The vote was 283 to 16. This bill received Royal Assent on March 25, 1807.

And the British slave trade was no longer legal.

Are you willing to be theatrical in your efforts to change your organization's culture?

CHAPTER EIGHT

Creating a Story Cascade

Your culture changes when old stories about the values and norms in your organization are replaced with new stories about new values and norms. You begin this change process when you build authentic stories that star you, that identify a clear break with the past and a path to the future, that appeal to both the head and heart, and that are theatrical in nature. These kinds of stories begin the culture-change process.

However, this process only creates a new culture when you are able to enroll other members of your organization in cocreating that culture with you. That happens when others in your organization start building their own culture-changing stories. This is what we call a story cascade. To the extent that these stories support and extend the stories you have built, then those that have built them are cocreating the new culture with you.

Story-Sharing Techniques

Of course, for a story cascade to emerge in your organization, your employees must first become aware of the culture-changing story or stories you have built. Stories that are not shared and discussed among your employees have no power to influence these people to build their own stories. In short—no story sharing, no story cascade. And no story cascade, no culture change.

Fortunately, our research suggests that there are a variety of techniques available for you to share the stories you build with members of your organization. Consider a few examples.

When a Story Shares Itself

Sometimes a story you build will share itself. It will be so compelling and built in such a way that it will spread throughout your organization like wildfire. This is particularly likely to happen when the story you build has all the attributes identified in this book.

Recall, for example, the first story we told in this book—Story 1.1 in Chapter 1—about Manoel Amorim inviting call center employees to explain to his executive team what information was needed in order to address service problems with a new product. This story was deeply authentic—since Manoel was convinced that his company needed to adopt a customer service culture to compete in its new environment. It also starred the business leader but was built in a public setting—namely, in the executive committee meeting at the firm. It marked a clear break with the past and a path to the future, appealed to both employee heads and hearts, and was deeply theatrical.

How long do you think it took for this story to spread throughout the organization? Hours? Minutes? Certainly, less than a day!

How long do you think it took for Jamie O'Banion's decision (Story 4.5) to go on television to sell her beauty products even though her eyebrow was split in two to be shared throughout her organization?

How long do you think it took the bread and water celebration created by Jeff Rodek (Story 7.1) to be shared throughout his organization?

These and many other stories presented in this book almost shared themselves. But this is not always the case. Sometimes you may have to take a more proactive approach in developing a strategy for sharing the stories you are building.

Using All-Hands Meetings to Build and Share Stories

Business leaders often use all-hands meetings to build and share culture-changing stories. These meetings can include everyone in an organization (e.g., Dan Burton at Health Catalyst—Story 3.5), everyone in a plant (a plant manager who took personal responsibility for a failed product—Story 4.3), or just those directly reporting to a business leader (Stefano Rettore at ADR—Story 3.3). In all these cases, the purpose of the all-hands event was not just to share some information, or to ask and answer questions. The purpose was to build culture-changing stories, stories that exemplified the kind of organizational cultures these business leaders were trying to implement.

Sometimes these all-hands events can be a very successful way to build and share a story. Consider the example of Cliff Clive, a business leader trying to transform the inefficient culture of his company.

STORY 8.1 "Stop Lifting the Pig"
Cliff Clive as CEO of MediNatura

When we were still a division of Heel Pharmaceuticals—a German homeopathic medicines firm—growing the US operation was a high priority. It was a global priority, and headquarters was spending money on the US business like a drunken sailor. They had built up this organization with almost 400 SKUs, with 120 employees, and were losing $5 million a year. Every month, we would spend more money than we made, and we would inform Germany, and they would just send us more money.

When I was asked to be general manager of the US operation, I knew that this was not a good way to build the business. So I called a company-wide meeting, and I began my talk with a joke. This joke has taken on a life of its own in our company. In fact, the punchline of this joke is used almost every day inside the company. It has become a touchstone of our culture—especially since we became an independent company.

Here's the joke. There once was a Swiss manager traveling through the United States. One day, he visited a farm and happened to watch how this particular farmer fed his pigs. What this farmer would do is pick up a pig and lift it high in the air so that the pig could eat apples from a tree. After one pig had eaten its fill of apples, the farmer would put it back on the ground, and lift up another pig, until all the pigs were fed.

This approach to feeding pigs offended the Swiss manager's preference for operational efficiency. "Listen, my friend," the manager said to the farmer. "Why don't you get a stick, knock several apples from the tree, let them fall to the ground, and then the pigs can eat the apples off the ground. It would take much less time." The Swiss visitor, satisfied that he had helped the farmer, turned and walked away. But the farmer was confused and said to himself, "Those crazy Swiss. What's time to a pig?"

After I told the joke, I went on: "Look. I'm at the top of the organization. I don't see 95 percent of what goes on in this company. But I can guarantee that every single one of you is spending time lifting pigs when we do things that were dictated to us by our German headquarters but make no sense here. And because we are spending all this time lifting pigs, we are losing money like crazy. What I need you to do is to look around this company, identify areas of inefficiency, and fix them. In other words, we need to stop lifting the pig."

So, when a team in our company is doing something because "that's the way it's always been done" or is a holdover from when we were part of the German firm, it is not unusual to hear people say, "Look, I think we're lifting the pig here." In fact, we have quarterly meetings where teams share how they are no longer "lifting the pig."

Clive identified a cultural problem in his company. He called an all-hands meeting to discuss this problem and its solution. Using the "lifting the pig" joke, he called for a clear break with the past, with a path toward the future. Moreover, the joke itself was theatrical. And Clive told the joke in this meeting—so he starred in the story he built. As the phrase "lifting the pig" spread throughout the company, it came to symbolize the new culture that Clive was trying to create. Every time someone used the line "we're lifting the pig here," they were participating in the cocreation of a new efficiency-oriented culture at the firm.

Using Small Group Meetings to Build and Share Stories

Sometimes the way that you share a story becomes part of the story you build. This approach to story building and sharing is an application of an idea first developed by Marshall McLuhan that suggests that "the medium is the message."[1] The "medium" in this context is the way that you share your story, while the "message" is the specific cultural content of your story. How you share your story (the medium) can actually become the content of your story (the message). Consider, for example, how the process that Pete Pizarro used to share his story helped reinforce the cultural content of that story.

STORY 8.2 "I Was the Student Our Company Was Designed to Serve" Pete Pizarro as CEO at Ilumno

People ask me how I ended up in the educational sector, first as the president and CEO at Whitney International University Systems—now known as Ilumno—and more recently as cofounder of SALT Venture Partners—a firm that facilitates investment in educational technology. This part of my career, and my approach to managing these educational firms, reflects my personal experiences growing up.

I was born in Cuba. I came as a political refugee to the United States when I was young, one year old. My father and my family were separated by the communist regime—my dad stayed behind in Cuba to help get his mother out, and my mom and her parents came to the United States. When we landed here, we got processed in a refugee processing center, and they gave us one-way tickets to California and Social Security cards. Everybody immediately went to work. Three years later, my dad was able to leave Cuba with his mother and join us in the United States.

I grew up for a while in Los Angeles but spent most of my childhood in Miami. I grew up in a very, very poor neighborhood, and went to a very rough high school. There was always fighting. I got into some trouble in high school but was able to graduate. After graduation, I was in bad company. I didn't think college was for me.

One night, me and my buddies were doing our thing and getting in trouble. But that particular night, I almost got arrested and almost went to jail. I woke up the next morning realizing how close things had come. Deep inside, I knew that that troublemaker wasn't really inside me. That was just me in the environment where I lived. That morning, I decided to go to Miami Dade Community College. They gave scholarships to potential students like me—very, very low-cost access to college. That night convinced me that I needed to change my life, and education was going to be the key.

While I was in community college, my grandfather got me a ticket to hear a speech by the president of the Federal Reserve. I was 18 years old at the time. The person I happened to sit next to at that speech headed up a scholarship fund for students to the University of Miami. He made it sound like someone like me could go to that university. So I got good grades at community college, applied for a scholarship, and was admitted to the University of Miami—even though I was from a very low-income background.

I graduated with a degree in accounting. I had maintained very good grades at Miami, so I was able to go to work at KPMG coming out of school. I hated every minute of that job because I was an auditor and I hated auditing. I had a lot of entrepreneurial ambitions. I didn't know what auditing was going to be like for sure, but counting other people's money wasn't my thing. So I left KPMG after a couple of years. I then had a series of very interesting and developmental jobs in IT and telecommunications and got an MBA at Northwestern. But I was always attracted to entrepreneurship and especially to the educational sector, because it had such an impact on my life.

In 2011, I was asked to be the CEO of Whitney International University Systems, now Ilumno. At the time, Ilumno had 10 universities located in 7 countries throughout Latin America. We had 155,000 degree-seeking students, 32 campuses, and over 8,000 academic and professional staff. Most of our students were the first members of their families to go to college. Most of them came from relatively poor backgrounds. In other words, most of our students were like me. By the way, the company now has over 300,000 students and 18 universities.

With an operation this large, it is easy for things to get bureaucratic, to treat students like they are just numbers, not real people with real potential. With my background, my story, I could not let this happen.

I had worked in companies where millions of dollars were spent on the best-known consultants, and still, people in the company did not understand the vision and strategy of the company. This could not happen in our firm. So I spent 80 percent of my time on the road, meeting and talking with students, faculty, and staff. I would pick the up-and-coming high-performing employees, and I would find employees who were influential in their organizations, and we would have breakfast. I would also meet with students in the same way.

Over breakfast, I would tell them my story. I would explain to them how my story led me to conclude that we're not here to enroll students. We were not going to refer to potential students as "leads." Our company doesn't focus on enrolling students. Our focus is on graduating students—to make sure that we keep them in the classroom, to make sure that we give them a quality education. If we graduate students, we will be successful and financially sustainable. And that was what I wanted people throughout the organization to understand, from the bottom up and from the top down.

To me, our mission was to democratize education and give every single underprivileged student an opportunity. I would always say, I'm the lucky one. Given where I came from, I was lucky. But we wanted to create a company where you don't have to be lucky to get access to education. And we contribute to a society where people like me—people who were going down the wrong path, who were doing the wrong things, who were just going all over town having fun and causing trouble—leave that behind, go to school, and then transform their lives.

What really made us have success is that everybody in the company knew our vision. Everybody knew our strategy, and everybody bought into it. And my personal story made it all real—one person, one breakfast at a time.

Pete's personal story was, of course, very moving—a classic "rags to riches" story. However, it became a culture-changing story for two reasons. First, the content of the story was linked to the strategy that Pete wanted to see implemented in his organization. That strategy seems simple enough—focus on educating and graduating students instead of simply enrolling students. And yet we have seen many for-profit universities and colleges focus all their efforts on recruiting students, and less effort on educating their students for the job market.[2] As his firm got larger and larger, it would have been easy to lose track of this educational mission, and Pete's story helped make the company's strategy and commitment clear.

But notice how the process by which Pete shared his story reinforced the message of his story. The core message of Pete's story is that each student must be treated as a unique individual, with unique potential, and never just as a "lead" to generate sales revenue. And how did Pete share this story? He spent 80 percent of his time traveling from campus to campus, meeting with students, faculty, and staff in small groups, often over breakfast. In effect, the way that Pete shared his story reinforced the central message of the story—just as I treat each of you, my students and employees, as individuals, so too I expect you to treat those with whom you interact—our current and potential students—as individuals, with individual worth. The results of this effort were substantial growth and financial success.

Sharing and Building Stories on the Web

How does the CEO of a web-based company help develop a culture that focuses on the excellence of a customer's experience on a firm's website? Using the web, of course.

STORY 8.3 "Screenshot Brett"
Brett Keller as CEO at Priceline

If you talk to employees at every level of the company, one of the things they'll tell you is that I'm famous for sending them screenshots of something on our website that doesn't function properly, or that I think could be improved. I'm a fanatical user of our products on all our platforms— desktop computers, mobile phones, iPads. I also use our competitor's products, as well as the demand channels that we use to get consumers into our experiences.

For example, I love to open Google at 2:00 a.m. on a Friday night and start typing in travel terms. Then I start clicking on ads to see where that's going to land me. I also start making travel reservations, and I start booking something. Anything I experience in those sessions that is not a seamless and frictionless experience for me as a consumer, I take a screenshot of it, and I send it to the product owner or the business partner who negotiated the deal. I'm giving this person feedback from my point of view as a consumer.

When these emails show up, the people in charge of this part of the product know that they don't have to get them fixed immediately. But they have to think about whether or not what I've identified is really a problem, and if it is, they need to get it fixed. They know that I love our product, that I spend as much time as I can on it. They know that we are on the same side—we want to make the consumer experience on our product as great as possible.

You know, it's very easy for people to get lost in their jobs and to lose track of what the consumer is actually experiencing. It's like you put blinders on—"My job is to negotiate great flight deals." That's great. We need that focus. But how often do you actually shop these deals on the website and try to push them onto different platforms? If you're not doing this, then you don't know how good the deal really is. Or if you're a product owner that owns the hotel experience, and you're responsible for how the room content shows up on the page, if you're not actually using the website as a product, where you are booking something for yourself, you'll never experience the product the right way. If you are always looking at a product as a product owner—you wrote a spec and gave it to a designer or developer and they've launched it—you may have checked all the technical boxes, but the consumer experience may be terrible.

What I'm trying to do is to instill in my people that to understand how the consumer experiences our product, you have to be a consumer. You can't be just the product owner or the business owner. The only way to do that is to use our product as a consumer. And the great thing about our services is that you can use them anywhere at any time.

So, for example, I use the product when I'm on vacation. In fact, I use our product every day. Every single day. Fortunately, I don't find problems every day, but I do send out screenshots at least once a week. And I've been doing this for 20 years, ever since I've been with the company.

Here is a specific example. We just launched a VIP program. In our first CEO meeting, I started by congratulating everybody for this incredible program. I showed them a screenshot of my VIP profile and I told them everything I liked about it. I also pointed to some things that I didn't like. For example, I thought there was some copy that wasn't written for someone who would be at the VIP level.

I'm not getting too deep into the weeds. I'm not telling my people how to fix the problems I identify, or even that they are really problems. All I'm doing is reacting to our products as a consumer—are they seamless and frictionless? If that is not my experience as a consumer, then our team needs to figure out how to address this issue.

Sometimes I think people might be afraid to get a screenshot from me. It's like they don't want to open their emails from me because, if they do, they'll see a screenshot that will force them to go to work to fix an issue. But I'm just like a consumer here, and if the consumer is experiencing this problem, then, yes, we do need to get it fixed.

I also don't skip levels in the organization when I give this consumer feedback. I send my screenshot to the person who is in charge of the particular part of our product I am evaluating. I don't want to undercut this person's authority by sending a screenshot to people who report to this person. In fact, this isn't about "catching someone" in a mistake or having a "gotcha moment." It's about making the best product we can.

This consumer-oriented culture has really caught on in the firm. Now when I send a screenshot, the response I often get is "Yeah, we're aware of this problem. It's already in the pipeline and we're going to fix it." We've gone from a world where our people generally did not use our product to a world where our people are expert consumers of our services. And because of this, the passion for the user experience has greatly improved.

Again, Brett's cultural message is very clear: we need to have the best consumer experience with our product possible. This is part of Priceline's product differentiation strategy in the very competitive online services industry. And the way that Brett communicates this message—the medium—is perfectly matched to the content of that message: he sends screenshots of parts of the online experience with his company's website that are not smooth or flawless. He uses these screenshots to communicate the importance of making the consumer experience on the website as flawless as possible.

Of course, each screenshot is likely only to make a small impact on the overall quality of the consumer experience at Priceline. But the story that he has built with multiple screenshots every week over many years is that the consumer experience at Priceline is sacred. It is the essential element of what makes Priceline special and a central value in its culture.

Sharing and Building Stories on the Phone

Sometimes the act of sharing is the story that is being built. Consider the experience of a chief manufacturing officer at a global firm.

> **STORY 8.4** "Caring for Employees during Covid"
> **The chief manufacturing officer of a giant global corporation**
>
> When things go badly, having established a culture of competence, character, and caring is very important. When I took over the supply chain for one of the company's large businesses, there wasn't a culture where management would spend enough time on the factory floor and really talk to people one on one about how things were going.
>
> Once I arrived, I decided to travel and visit at least one factory or technical center a week. I switched my entire schedule to spend 70 to 80 percent of my time out in the operations and the rest at headquarters. Through that process, I got to know the people in our operations, and they got to know me and that I was concerned for them.
>
> And then many years later Covid happened. The first thing we did, of course, was to focus on competence—we wanted to make the people in our plants as safe as possible. So we built safety protocols in a week and then implemented them.

Then we focused on the character and caring parts of our culture. In particular, I spent a lot of time connecting casually with every leader in the factories, especially those on the factory floor. For example, at that time, we had over 100 plant managers. I called each one of these people individually, without pre-announcing the phone calls, just to ask how they were doing. I spent 30 minutes talking with each of these leaders.

Most of the time, when they got this kind of phone call, it was to ask about a problem or to ask for some data or information. This time, my phone call with them was "Hey, here I am. What can I do to help? How are you feeling? How is your family?"

That was over 100 phone calls, but it sent an unmistakable message that I and the company care about each of these people, and each of the people who worked in this division.

Over 100 phone calls. Each lasting about 30 minutes. Do the math—that is approximately 50 hours of phone calls! It almost didn't matter what this leader said on each of these phone calls—the *act of calling all his people was the message*. It was a message about the kind of culture he wanted in his organization, despite the pandemic.

Limits to Your Story-Sharing Strategy

All these examples show that sharing the stories you build is an important part of the culture-change process. But sharing your stories can also create problems. This happens when how you share your story undercuts the authenticity of your story.

Consider the stories shared with us by Mike Staffieri—where he visited an employee whose wife was undergoing cancer surgery and an employee who had just had a baby (Story 6.4). These were deeply personal, even intimate stories, that reflected Mike's individual commitment to live the values of the culture at DaVita.

But what would have happened if Mike had broadly shared these stories at an all-hands meeting or on a website? In broadly communicating these stories himself, they would suddenly have appeared as deeply self-serving and manipulative—"Look at me, look how good a person I am" or "Look at me, look how well I live the DaVita values." The stories themselves would not have changed, but their meaning would be entirely different. Instead of reaffirming DaVita's culture, they would have undermined it.

So, Mike's sharing strategy was to not share. Not sharing meant that the culture-changing implications of these stories could not be realized—at least not by Mike. However, this was better than aggressively sharing these stories in a way that undermined the DaVita culture.

Of course, these kinds of stories almost always get out. They get shared. In Mike's case, the people whom he had served shared these experiences on their own, without any prompting or encouragement. They shared these stories—in one case at a large meeting and in another case through informal social networks—because, in a real sense, they had to. They had to because what Mike did in living DaVita's values had such a personal impact on them. And they shared those stories in a way that not only recognized Mike's role but reinforced the culture at DaVita.

One for all, and all for one!

Building Story Cascades

Sharing the stories you have built makes it possible to create a story cascade in your organization. A story cascade exists when people in your organization build their own stories, stories that support and even extend the story or stories you have built. In building their own stories, these individuals help cocreate a new culture in your organization.

We already know that story building can be personally risky and challenging for you as a business leader. It can be even more risky and challenging—indeed, downright scary—for people throughout your organization. What can you do to encourage others in your organization to build their own stories, so that as an organization, you can create a story cascade?

Build More Stories

One reason your employees may be unwilling to build their own stories is because they are unsure of your commitment to culture change. Sure, you built a wonderful first story. But is it a one-off? Or are you really committed to culture change?

Answer this question by building another story. And this new story should have all the attributes of your first story, the attributes described in this book.

Not only will this new story reassure your employees that you are actually committed to changing your organization's culture, it will also give you an opportunity to further articulate the values, beliefs, and norms that you think are going to be important in this new culture. Recall that you will often begin the culture-change process with an incomplete vision of the culture you are trying to build in your organization. You need to know the general direction of this culture-change effort—we need a more innovation-friendly culture, a more consumer-oriented culture, a more transparent culture—but many of the details of this culture will not be fully specified.

This, of course, is actually a good thing and can help make the culture-change process successful. This is because by keeping many of the details of the culture you are trying to create unspecified, you are creating room for your employees to cocreate this culture with you. This helps avoid the top-down and dictatorial feelings that can emerge when a business leader announces the need for a new culture, specifies what its four (or is it three or five?) core values will be, and lists the kinds of behaviors that will and will not be acceptable in this new culture. The process of cocreating your culture with your employees may ultimately lead to such clear lists of values and expected behaviors, but it is typically better to let these emerge over time rather than to try to impose them on your organization from the beginning.

That said, with only a single culture-changing story to hang on to, your employees will probably need more guidance and insight with regard to the kind of culture you are trying to build. Rather than describing this culture in some abstract way, as a list of values or norms that could short-circuit the culture cocreation process, build another culture-changing story. This way, not only will you have a continuing impact on the content of the new culture you are building in your firm, you will do so in a way that encourages culture cocreation with your employees.

Ask Critical Managers to Build Their Own Stories

You can build your culture-changing stories, and then wait and hope that other employees in your organization will begin to build their own stories.

Alternatively, you may want to ask certain influential and visible members of your organization to build their own stories. In doing so, you might want to suggest the attributes of a story that make it more likely to change your organization's culture. We call this "story seeding"—and it can generate a bountiful harvest of culture-changing stories.

Of course, the culture-changing story your employees build must be their story. It cannot be a story you build for them. If they share a culture-changing story that is not their own, it would not be authentic. If employees in your organization build inauthentic culture-changing stories, these stories can be easily dismissed as cynical attempts to "suck up" to the business leader.

Celebrate Stories Built by Your Employees

Whether stories emerge on their own or because you have seeded them, when they happen, celebrate them. Tell them to everyone you see, in every meeting you attend, in every speech you give. Consider the role of celebrating the stories built by employees at Traeger, a firm in the outdoor cooking market.

Jeremy Andrus—CEO of Traeger—had bought a firm with a toxic culture. Convinced that this company's unique pellet-based smoking system could disrupt the mature outdoor cooking industry, Jeremy had become equally convinced that his company would not be able to exploit this opportunity with their current culture.

Jeremy tried to change Traeger's culture, but ultimately decided that he would have to build a new culture from scratch. So Jeremy fired almost all of his employees and moved the company's headquarters from Oregon to Utah.[3]

In this process, Jeremy built some compelling stories about the kind of innovative and consumer-oriented culture he wanted at Traeger. But he still wasn't sure that this culture change was spreading throughout the company. And then this happened.

> **STORY 8.5 "No Reservation Customer Service"**
> **Jeremy Andrus as CEO at Traeger Pellet Grills**
>
> We have five core values in the culture we have created at Traeger. One of them is "no reservations." What "no reservations" is about is not just fix-

ing a moment for our customers, but it's having no reservations about creating an experience that's meaningful to a customer. Our brand purpose is to bring people together around meaningful food experiences. The grill is a means to that end. So, for us, our job is to help our customers have those meaningful food experiences, with no reservations on our part. I remember the first time I saw this commitment to "no reservations" in action.

I was in my office on a Monday morning. My head of sales comes into my office and says, "You're not going to believe what Rob did over the weekend!" I couldn't wait to hear. He tells me this story: Rob—he was a junior guy in our organization—gets a phone call from an assistant warehouse manager of a Costco in Seattle. This manager says, "Hey, I'm sorry. I didn't know who else to call. It's Friday night, I'm cooking a big brisket and having people over for game day tomorrow, and my Traeger won't start!"

So, Rob is a young guy. He's got his first child at home—like eight weeks old—and has every reason to hand this off to someone else or to say, "I'll call you back on Monday." Instead, he said, "Okay, let's diagnose the problem right now. Walk me through what's going on. What's happening?" After a few minutes, Rob says, "I think I know what's going on." He validates his diagnosis, then he buys a plane ticket, goes to the office on the way to the airport, picks up the component he needs—the auger isn't working correctly—flies to Seattle from Salt Lake City, goes to the customer's home, fixes the machine, turns it on, helps the customer season his brisket, starts the cooking process, gets on a plane, and heads back to Utah.

Then Rob comes in Monday morning like nothing special has happened—just sits there working on a spreadsheet, doing his work. He didn't raise his hand and say, "Hey, guys, guess what I did?" Instead, he felt empowered to buy the ticket and go fix the guy's grill, so that is what he did. He was just doing his job. No big deal. In the old culture, he would have been fired for buying an airplane ticket without asking someone first.

So, this is how we heard about what Rob did: The Costco warehouse assistant manager with the broken grill told his manager about Rob, who called the merchant at Costco corporate, who told his VP, who called my head of sales—and by noon on Monday, our head of sales walked into my office to tell me what Rob did.

After I heard this story, all I said was, "It's working. This is exactly what I want to have happen." It wasn't just that Rob fixed a customer's problem. It wasn't even that he went to Seattle to fix it. It's that he did this on his own—that he felt empowered to live the value of "no reservations." Interestingly, Rob was one of the few people who came from the old Traeger office in Oregon. There was no way he would have done this in the old Traeger culture.

This is the beginning of a story cascade.

Interestingly, Rob didn't know that he was building a story—he was just doing his job in a way that was consistent with Traeger's new culture. But as soon as Jeremy heard what Rob had done, he instantly recognized that Rob had built his own story, a story that helped exemplify the culture that Jeremy wanted to create. And, almost immediately, Jeremy found a way to share this new story throughout the company.

Story 8.6 "Building on an Employee's Commitment to Service" Jeremy Andrus as CEO at Traeger Pellet Grills

What Rob had done was amazing. But he didn't know how important it actually was. He just came back into work, sat down at his computer, and did his work. He didn't raise his hand or brag about what he did. After all, he had just done what he thought was expected of him.

But I wanted to celebrate his story. Based on what Rob did and our belief that recognizing cultural contributions drives positive behaviors, we decided to create a program called "Value Our Values." Every quarter, peers get to recognize peers for living a cultural value—a very specific thing they have observed. They get a chance to get $100 from the company for every person they recognize—just to motivate them to do it.

What we've learned is that when a leader recognizes someone for living the values, it feels good, and it creates a sense of job security for the one being recognized. But when a peer recognizes a peer, the person who's been recognized feels this overwhelming sense of purpose, like they have added something to the culture and the mission of the organization.

Now we receive hundreds of peer-to-peer recognitions. I read all of these peer-to-peer recognitions. I created this program because I wanted people like Rob to be recognized for living our values, without ever having to raise their hand.

I can tell you that it's fun to put $400 or $500 dollars in an envelope and give it to people who have recognized their peers for living our values. Some of these envelopes are thick with Benjamins.

We do this quarterly, but each Monday morning we also have an all-hands meeting where I share examples of people in the firm living our values. It is great to recognize these people publicly.

What Jeremy realized is that not only was story sharing important for the stories he built, it was also important for the stories that others in his organization built.

Manoel Amorim, at Telesp, also understood the importance of celebrating stories being built throughout his organization. Consider his multipronged approach to creating a story cascade in his company.

STORY 8.7 "Celebrating Story Building"
Manoel Amorim as CEO at Telesp (Telefonica)

During my first year as CEO, we decided to start collecting customer service stories in our organization. Every top executive was invited to submit a story that he or she thought was worth sharing. This would happen in our weekly executive meeting. We then would choose three or four of these stories that we thought would be worth sharing throughout the company.

Then we would publish these stories in our monthly newsletter, along with photos of the people who had built these stories. For example, in one newsletter we featured a story from sales about a woman who took it upon herself to analyze potential customer satisfaction issues in the sales process and fix them; a story about six guys who built a training lab—at no cost—to train every customer service representative in the call center about how our product worked, from the central station and servers to the consumers' home; and four guys who created and tested a process to minimize vandalism on our public phones.

In addition, I personally picked one to three stories every month and visited, face to face, the person or people who had built the stories, to thank them. Sometimes they were invited to have lunch with me to tell me how they had done it and what was next for them. This had a tremendous motivation effect in the organization.

Finally, we created something we called the "Race of the Champions." This was a competition that carried a sizable prize. Everybody could participate. The process consisted of identifying a project that would achieve good results under the race's theme, propose it to their supervisor (who was expected to help and mentor the respective team), implement it, and then measure its impact. They would then submit the project, and a committee would evaluate and rank them.

In our annual meeting we would recognize the winners and hand out the prizes. The first prize was a check for USD $10,000, which was a lot of money for these employees.

During my time as CEO, we launched four races with the following themes: cost reduction, customer satisfaction A, customer satisfaction B, and employee satisfaction. By the third wave of those races, 70 percent of the workforce had implemented a project of their own initiative. In that third wave alone, there were about 8,000 story builders in the competition. As the year progressed, we would feature some of these stories in the monthly newsletter.

Conclusion

There may come a time in your career where the opportunity to build and the opportunity to share a culture-changing story are perfectly aligned. In these moments, your actions can have a profound effect on the culture of your organization.

Such a moment for the culture of the United States occurred on August 28, 1963, in front of the Lincoln Memorial in Washington, D.C., before an audience of over 250,000 people. In that moment, Dr. Martin Luther King Jr. built and shared a vision of race relations that affected and continues to affect societies and cultures around the world. Often called the "I Have a Dream" speech, King not only shared a vision about what could be but also how we could all become part of making this ideal real.

As an example of public speaking, it was a masterstroke. Drawing on his experience as a preacher in the Baptist Church, King used anaphora—repeating the same phrase or sentence in a speech to drive home and give emphasis to a point—to near perfection. Referring to the Emancipation Proclamation, King began his speech with four sentences, each beginning with "One hundred years later . . ." He then started two sentences with "We refuse to believe . . . ," followed by four sentences that started with "Now is the time . . ." and seven sentences that started with "We can never be satisfied. . . ." Encouraging his audience to take action when they returned home, he began the next six sentences in his speech with "Go back. . . ."

Then the eight sentences that still give us hope and pause, all of which began with "I have a dream. . . ." Following these, three sentences that started "With this faith . . ." and a conclusion of nine sentences—a call to action that resonates down through the years—that all began with "Let freedom ring. . . ."

He also used metaphors and the language of contrasts to help make his points. His first words—"Four score years ago"—were a clear reference to Lincoln's Gettysburg address. His language "joyous daybreak to end this long night of their captivity" and "sweltering with the heat of oppression, will be transformed into an oasis of freedom and justice" used comparisons between contrasting states to highlight differences between what was and what could be in race relations.

And Dr. King also presented his speech so well—with his melodic baritone voice rising and falling as he punctuated certain words and phrases for emphasis.

It was musical.

But with all this masterful writing and speaking, the speech would not have had much impact if it was not authentic to the man Martin Luther King Jr. Indeed, he had earned the right to give that speech—in 1955, he joined the bus boycott in Montgomery, Alabama, after Rosa Parks had refused to move to the back of the bus; in 1957, he organized the Southern Christian Leadership Conference, a leader in the civil rights movement; in 1960, he was arrested at a protest in a segregated restaurant in Atlanta; in 1962, he was arrested for protesting in Albany, Georgia; in 1963, he was arrested in Birmingham, Alabama, where he spent 11 days in jail; and later that year, he led a march of 125,000 people on a Freedom Walk in Detroit. And all this time, he preached nonviolent but active protest.

Even with this background, the setting for making this speech was not perfect. He was originally given four minutes on the program. He spoke for 16 minutes. Almost no one in the audience could hear him—the public address system had been sabotaged. The "I Have a Dream" part of the speech was improvised. He had given a version of that speech previously, but those words were not included in his prepared remarks. Then, partway through his speech, singer and activist Mahalia Jackson shouted out "Tell them about the dream, Martin!" King responded. And the rest, as they say, is history.

Obviously, the "I Have a Dream" speech is a very high bar for evaluating your ability to build and share culture-changing stories in your organization. But the attributes of that speech that made it so impactful—its authenticity, its masterful delivery, its clean break with the past with a clear path to the future, its appeal to our heads and hearts, and its theatricality—are the same attributes that your stories must have if they are to change your organization's culture. If you build these kinds of stories, they will be told and retold throughout your organization—creating the story cascade that will change your organization's culture.

Are you willing to build and share culture-changing stories in your firm?

CHAPTER NINE

Making Culture Change Stick

B uilding stories is the beginning of the culture-change process. But it is more than that—it is the soul of the culture-change process. Then creating a story cascade broadens culture change by engaging your people in cocreating your new culture. Story cascades ensure that the culture that is created is not just yours but is owned by your entire organization.

But making culture change stick moves beyond building stories, and beyond even creating a story cascade. Making culture change stick is likely to require you to change other policies and practices in your organization, policies and practices that may be inconsistent with the culture you are trying to create.

When you align these other policies and practices with the culture you are creating, your culture-change efforts are likely to have more staying power. If you fail to create this alignment, your existing policies and practices will constantly gnaw at and undermine the new culture you are trying to create. At the very least, your employees will be confused about the direction of your organization—are you implementing a new culture or are you maintaining policies and practices that undermine this new culture? At worst, some of your employees may use existing policies and practices that contradict your culture-change efforts to justify resisting those efforts. Why should they take culture-change efforts seriously when you are still implementing policies and practices that are clearly inconsistent with the new culture?

Why Past Policies and Practices Are Often Not Aligned with a New Culture

Of course, not all your current policies and practices will conflict with the culture you are trying to build. However, it is not unusual for some of these conflicts to exist. This is because your past policies and practices are often aligned with your old culture, and thus are often misaligned with the new culture. This is especially likely if there are fundamental differences between your old and new cultures.

For example, if your old culture emphasized individual contributions more than teamwork, then your employee evaluation and compensation policies are more likely to focus on measuring individual performance than measuring team performance. If your old culture emphasized functional competence in hiring new employees over the ability of new employees to cooperate cross-functionally, then your hiring policies are more likely to focus on hiring the smartest engineers, or the most careful accountants, or the most creative marketing people, rather than hiring people who can cooperate across functions to implement your strategies. If your old culture emphasized efficiently executing a plan more than creatively developing a plan, then your current policies and practices are more likely to focus on managerial execution than on managerial creativity.

None of these policies or practices are, by themselves, problematic. They only become a problem when your current policies and practices are inconsistent with your new culture. Thus, if the new culture you are building values teamwork, cross-functional cooperation, and creativity, and your current policies are inconsistent with these values, you will need to change your policies and practices.

Which Policies and Practices Will You Need to Change?

Even relatively small organizations have hundreds of policies and practices. Larger organizations can have hundreds of pages of policy and practices manuals. Which of these policies and practices will most likely need to be changed to align them with your new culture?

While any particular policy might need to be changed in your efforts to create a new culture in your organization, our research shows that the kinds of policies that are most likely to require this kind of change are human resource policies—how your organization hires, trains, evaluates, compensates, and terminates its employees. HR policies and practices are often where the values and norms of the culture you are trying to create become operationalized.

On their own, these values and norms can be quite abstract and theo-retical. This is one reason why just posting lists of new cultural values in your organization is such an ineffective way of creating culture change. However, they are made more concrete by the stories you build that exem-plify these values and norms. They become even more concrete by the stories that are built throughout your organization in a story cascade.

But it is when these new values and norms alter the way that people are hired, trained, evaluated, compensated, and terminated throughout your organization that their implications for your employees become most clear. Teamwork is abstract until your employees are evaluated on their team con-tributions; cross-functional cooperation is abstract until your employees are trained how to cooperate across functions; creativity is abstract until some of your employees are promoted because of their creativity.

Hiring Practices

From the point of view of making your cultural change stick, your hiring practices must not only focus on hiring employees sufficiently competent to do the tasks they are hired to do, they must also have values that are con-sistent with the new culture you are trying to create.

Of course, firms have long been hiring new employees based on their business skills and competencies. Over the years, the best human resource professionals have learned how to identify the business skills and compe-tencies that are required to do a job, and how to determine whether or not a potential employee has these skills and competencies. In fact, the more competent your HR staff is, the more skilled they are likely to be in this competence-based approach to hiring.[1]

However, hiring employees based on how their values relate to the cul-ture you are trying to create may be new to your organization. Of course, this doesn't mean that employee skills and competencies are irrelevant in your hiring decisions, only that the ability of a potential employee to help in the implementation of a new culture is also important.

Your HR managers might reasonably ask how they are supposed to mea-sure and evaluate the cultural competence of potential employees. Great question, to which there is probably no single answer—if only because dif-ferent firms will seek to create different kinds of organizational cultures, which will require different measures to evaluate the values of potential employees. We do know of some firms that use case studies and simulations to evaluate a potential employee's values and how they fit with a company's new culture. We know of other firms that have defined the core values of their culture relative to a typology of personality types derived from psychological research, and then evaluated the values of potential employees using measures taken from this research.[2]

However your HR people end up measuring the values of potential employees and relating these to the culture you are trying to create, the main point is simple: Technical and functional skills and competencies are important in making hiring decisions. But when you are trying to change an organization's culture, you also need to hire based on the relationship between a potential employee's values and the culture you are trying to create.

In this context, a reasonable question is: If we hire based on values, won't we end up hiring people who are mostly like us? What happens to diversity in this context? In fact, the whole point of hiring people whose values are consistent with the culture you are trying to create is to hire people who have values that are enshrined in this culture. While it may not be "politically correct" to say this, when it comes to changing an organization's culture, extreme value diversity is often not helpful.

For example, if the cultural value you are trying to create is, say, increased transparency, and you hire a large number of technically competent employees who are not transparent, you will just confuse your organization. Such confusion can undermine your efforts to change your organization's culture.

Of course, the best world to be in is to hire technically competent people who have the values you are trying to install in your new organizational culture. But what if these people don't exist? What should you compromise on—technical competence or values? Our research suggests that—if forced to make this choice—organizations that are trying to build their competitive advantage based on their culture will compromise on technical competence before they compromise on employee values. That is, they are willing to sacrifice "one unit" of technical competence for "one unit" of cultural compatibility.

And in doing so, they will generate more economic value than would otherwise be the case.[3]

Of course, if you take this approach, you will need to be careful that you are not unintentionally screening out gender, racial, or other kinds of diversity in your hiring practices. The search for employees who have the values that you are trying to build into your new culture cannot become an excuse for failing to hire a diverse workforce. Indeed, that potential employees look and talk like you does not necessarily mean that they have the same cultural values as you. Hiring practices have to look beyond these superficial indicators of cultural affinity to deeper indicators of the values that potential employees hold dear, and how those values are related to the culture you are trying to implement in your organization.

Training Practices

Our experience suggests an interesting correlation between the extent to which a firm relies on its organizational culture to implement its strategies and the amount and nature of its training efforts. In general, the more an organization relies on its culture to implement its strategies, the more employee training the organization invests in and the more culturally oriented this training becomes.

For example, in the 1980s, when Hewlett-Packard was widely known for its distinctive and powerful organizational culture, that culture—described in a pamphlet titled "The HP Way"—took center stage in corporate training.[4] Over many years, Johnson & Johnson has tried to build its culture around a statement of values called "The Credo." To reinforce the importance of the Credo, some CEOs at J&J have traveled throughout the company, holding Credo training meetings with employees where they discuss the Credo and its implications for what was expected of J&J employees.[5] At Koch Industries, corporate training focuses on introducing market-like mechanisms into that organization's hierarchical organizational structure, in a way consistent with the organization values espoused by the CEO, Charles Koch.[6]

Of course, perhaps the most extreme examples of this focus on value-based training is found in the military, where units that rely completely on their members' ability to trust the competence and character of their colleagues—units like the Navy SEALS and the Army Rangers—go to extreme lengths to create a common culture during their training.[7]

It follows from this work that if you are trying to change your organizational culture, you will need to adopt similar kinds of culture-oriented elements in your employee training. Sure, it's important for your people to know all about their health care and other benefits. They should understand your organizational structure and your overall strategy. But even more importantly, they need to understand what is expected of them as a member of your organization. They need to understand the kind of culture you are trying to build in your organization and their role in creating this culture.

Practically speaking, such training should probably feature many of the stories that you and your employees have built to change your culture.

Employee Evaluation Practices

Every organization we know has practices and policies for evaluating the performance of their employees. Indeed, the performance of virtually every employee in an organization—from the CEO to the hourly worker in a plant—is evaluated. These evaluations are then used to adjust compensation levels and make decisions about promotions, demotions, and even terminations.

That said, business leaders sometimes forget that their approach to evaluating employee performance can say a great deal about their organization's culture. What you measure about your employees' performance speaks about what you and your organization value in employee performance. If you measure employees in ways that are inconsistent with the culture you are trying to create, you will almost certainly have to change your employee evaluation practices if you are going to make your culture-change efforts stick.

Consider how Manoel Amorim—the CEO of Telesp first mentioned in Chapter 1—used changes in employee evaluation practices to help implement his culture change. Recall that this Brazilian phone company was moving from a regulated monopoly to a more competitive market where customer satisfaction was going to be a competitive necessity. But everything about Telesp—including how it evaluated its employees—was aligned with the command-and-control culture that valued technical excellence and execution and that had served the company so well in its regulated market.

Of course, Manoel began the culture-change process by building a story (Story 1.1). He also did things to encourage the creation of a story cascade in the company (Story 8.7). But he still needed to change his company's HR policies, and that began with employee evaluations.

> **Story 9.1** "Bringing Customer Satisfaction into Employee Evaluation"
> **Manoel Amorim as CEO at Telesp (Telefonica)**
>
> We needed to align our employee evaluation system with our new culture. The first thing we did was to implement scorecards to clarify what was expected from each employee, at all levels in the company. There were clear and easy to measure goals for each of the components on the scorecard. And for the first time in the history of the company, "Customer Satisfaction" was part of everybody's scorecards.
>
> Then we implemented a 360-degree evaluation system—where each employee in the firm was provided feedback from his/her boss, subordinates, peers, and key clients. Coming from a very hierarchical organization, having subordinates evaluate their bosses was an important breakthrough.
>
> This 360-degree process brought fear initially, and several of my own direct reports mentioned they were not very comfortable with it. So I built another story: I decided to be the first one to be evaluated this way. When my results came back—and they were not 100 percent good—I called a meeting with all my direct reports, their direct reports, and their direct reports' direct reports. The company auditorium was full, with almost 1,000 seats taken. I shared with them the results of my 360-degree evaluation—what I was doing well, where I was falling short, and what my plan was to improve where I was falling short.
>
> The audience was shocked: "Can the CEO be evaluated by other people in the company now?" But they quickly realized the benefits of this approach to employee evaluation. After this meeting, this process cascaded down the organization and much of the fear was taken away as they saw me go through this process and went through it themselves. In just a couple of years, this evaluation time was something that people throughout the organization actually anticipated.

Both of the changes that Manoel made to employee evaluation at Telesp helped build the cooperative customer service–oriented culture he was trying to implement. First, he held everyone in the company accountable for customer satisfaction; second, he used the 360-degree evaluation process to show that every employee was important in the new Telesp—even low-level employees had the opportunity to evaluate their supervisors. And to facilitate the implementation of these two changes, Manoel built a story by publicly sharing the results of his own 360-degree evaluations.

Some of the measures you currently use to evaluate the performance of managers can be modified to include items that focus on culture-change efforts inside your firm. We saw this in Dan Burton's use of employee surveys, 360-degree employee evaluations, and direct feedback from individual employees about culture-change efforts at Health Catalyst (Story 3.5). Alberto Carvalho at Gillette used the willingness of product development teams to get out into the field to see how customers were actually using their product as a way to measure how committed particular R&D teams were to a new product innovation process (Story 4.4). And Jeremy Andrus used the actions of his employee to address customer problems "without reservation" as a measure of this employee's commitment to a new culture (Story 8.5).

Employee Compensation Practices

Of course, the logical consequence of changing employee evaluation is changing how employee compensation is set. Consider how Manoel altered compensation at Telesp.

STORY 9.2 "Compensating the Top Performers"
Manoel Amorim as CEO at Telesp (Telefonica)

Our new employee evaluation system made it possible to adjust our employee compensation policies. Based on employee scorecards and the results of the 360-degree review process, every single employee in the company was ranked. I ranked my VPs, my VPs ranked their directors, directors ranked their managers, and so forth, until every employee had been ranked on a forced curve.

Other than me, this ranking exercise was conducted by groups—that is, all the 50 directors were ranked by the 8 VPs. Then these 50 directors broke into groups to rank their subordinates, and so forth. These groups were all multifunctional in nature.

Each group had to come to a consensus on who were the top 20 percent, who were the bottom 20 percent, and who were the other 60 percent. There

was debate, multifunctional disagreements, collaboration, and conflict resolution. And everybody was ranked by the end of the process.

There were obvious consequences of these rankings. Nobody could fire
the top 20 percent. If a department closed—and that happened a number
of times—the department head or his/her supervisor had to find another
job in the company for those in the top 20 percent. Interestingly, there was
competition for that talent. People were beginning to trust the process.

The top 20 percent also received a bonus above their maximum pay
grade, paid by the bottom 20 percent of the performance curve, who received no bonus, no matter how well the company had done.

All these changes in how employees were compensated helped reinforce the
cooperative customer service–oriented culture that Manoel was trying to
implement.

Employee Termination Practices

Finally, the reality is that implementing culture change often will require
you to terminate some of your employees. What is even more difficult, some
of these employees may be performing at a high level in the old culture. But
if the way they get this high level of performance is inconsistent with the
new culture you are trying to create, you may still need to let them go.

We completely understand that this may not be fair. After all, these employees are simply doing what has been expected of them by the old culture. And now you are changing the rules of the game on them by changing
your organization's culture to more effectively implement new strategies.
It's like they signed up to play baseball—and have become proficient at that
game—and now you want them to start playing ice hockey!

Of course, they are going to feel lied to and exploited and manipulated.
Because, in one way, they have been lied to, exploited, and manipulated. In
fact, at least some of your employees were probably attracted to work for
your company precisely because they liked the old culture. And now the
very thing that attracted them to your firm in the first place is going away.
It's a classic bait and switch. While acknowledging their anger and frustration, it is important that you do not let these employees prevent you from
changing your organization's culture. Of course, you can reach out to these
people, explain what you are doing and why you are doing it. You can

invite them to become part of the new culture. Who knows—some of these employees may have been secretly waiting for the opportunity to help build a new culture in the firm. Others will make a business decision and get on board with the culture change. But others may resist this change and—either actively or passively—work to undermine your culture-change efforts. It is this last group that you will need to let go.

Using language from Jim Collins, culture change is usually an "on the bus" issue.[8] "On the bus" issues are generally so important and so central to an organization and its future that if managers are not willing to support you regarding these issues, then they will need to find alternative employment.

Firing these employees may actually be very freeing for at least some of them. A person who has been fully socialized into an old culture may feel very uncomfortable if and when that old culture is replaced. They may feel, as this new culture is implemented, that they no longer understand their role, that they no longer have a clear sense of the firm's purpose, that they no longer know how to work with others in the firm. And all of this is correct. Changing an organization's culture can change all these elements of a person's job and can leave them with a feeling of being lost and confused.

Sociologists have a name for this state of affairs: anomie—the state of normlessness. Culture change often creates a state of anomie among some employees. Some of these employees may be able to change and adapt to a firm's new culture and leave this sense of anomie behind. But others can't. For those who cannot change, separating from the firm can be a blessing. We saw this in the story of Steve Young firing the former CEO of a company his firm had purchased (Story 3.6).

Finally, deciding to fire some of your employees may not only have a direct impact on your ability to change your organization's culture, it may also be the source of particularly influential culture-changing stories. For example, if a top manager in your firm is widely seen as aggressively resisting your culture-change efforts, firing that employee sends an unmistakable message to the entire company about just how serious you are about implementing a new culture. This is especially the case if, along other important dimensions, this manager is performing effectively.

We once asked a senior manager we knew, who had been given the task of changing the culture of a well-known retail chain in the United States, what mistakes he had made in that process. His answer surprised us: "I should have instantly fired the five or six of my direct reports that I knew—on day one—would undermine our culture-change efforts. Instead, I waited a year to fire them, and this cost us a year in realizing our culture-change goals."

When to Align Your Organization with Your New Culture

Economists have a favorite saying: "Incentives work." What this means is that if you, as a business leader, want to change how your workers behave, change how you evaluate and compensate their performance. If you want more cooperation, measure and compensate cooperation. If you want more functional excellence, measure and compensate functional excellence. If you want more creativity, measure and compensate creativity.

Using language developed in Chapter 2, this is a very top-down and economically rational approach to managing change. And this approach may work for implementing a variety of organizational changes.

But not for changing an organization's culture.

As was suggested in Chapter 2, organizational culture has a variety of characteristics that suggest that any one approach to managing change—top-down or bottom-up, personal and emotional or rational and economic, or a systems approach to change—is not likely to be successful in changing an organization's culture. In that chapter, we suggested that you will need to adopt an *eclectic model of organizational change*, an approach that borrows change management techniques from a variety of models.

So, changing how you measure and compensate your employees may be part of changing your culture, but it is not the only thing. In particular, if you try to change your HR practices as a way to *create* culture change, you are almost certainly doomed to fail. Until your people understand the need for culture change, the nature of that change, and until they see your irreversible commitment to culture change, they are not likely to become part of the process of cocreating this new culture. And if they don't become part of the culture-change process, changes in your organizational policies and practices—by themselves—are not likely to create "sticky" culture change.

Thus, until you start building authentic stories in which you star, that mark a clear break with the past with a path to the future, that appeal to your employees' heads and hearts, are often theatrical, and are shared throughout your organization in ways that create a story cascade, then changing your HR policies is premature. After all, the point of changing your HR policies is to align them to the culture you are trying to build, but you only know what that culture will be once you begin the culture-change process and enroll your people to cocreate that new culture with you.

Of course, this doesn't mean that your culture change must be complete before you align your organization's policies and practices with a new culture. Indeed, creating this alignment can send a signal of just how serious you are about culture change. And as we have seen for Manoel at Telesp, this alignment process can also be a source of new culture-changing stories. But culture change begins with story building, matures with story cascades, and becomes "sticky" when your policies and practices are modified to be consistent with your new culture.

Conclusion

This, then, concludes our introduction to culture change. This process begins when you, as a business leader, note a misalignment between your strategies, what they are and how they are likely to evolve, and your organizational culture. It continues when you build one or more culture-changing stories with the attributes described in this book. Your change efforts begin to ripen when you share the stories you and your employees have built throughout your organization. This story cascade is the way that your people cocreate the new culture with you. Then, at some point, you analyze whether your current policies and practices are aligned with this new culture. If this is not the case, then you will have to change these policies and practices in a way that increases the chance that your culture change will actually stick.

This is the culture-change process. How you can start to implement this process—as soon as tomorrow—is discussed in the next chapter.

CHAPTER TEN

How to Build Your Own Culture-Changing Stories

S o, you want to change your culture.

To get to this point, you have probably concluded that you need to change your organization's strategies—the actions your organization takes to try to gain competitive advantage. You have also probably concluded that the new strategies you want to implement are not aligned with your existing culture. Faced with the choice between ignoring this misalignment and changing your culture, you have decided to try to change your culture.

Based on the research reported in this book, changing your organization's culture typically begins by building new stories to replace the old stories that exist in your old culture. Indeed, this book has described in some detail the attributes of stories that other business leaders have built to begin their own culture-changing process.

But how do you take these ideas and apply them in building your own story for your own organization?

Of course, we cannot tell you the specific stories you should build to change your organization's culture—those need to be authentic to you as a business leader and highly customized to your organization and its business challenges. However, our research does have some important implications for how you can build your own culture-changing story. We have framed these implications in a series of questions, summarized in Table 10.1.

Where Do Culture-Changing Stories Come From?

It has been suggested that all writing is autobiographical.[1] This is certainly true for the culture-changing stories you build. They almost always start with some experience you have had as a business leader—often with some aspect of your culture that is inconsistent with the strategy or strategies that

TABLE 10.1	Practical Guides for Building Your Own Culture-Changing Stories

1. Where do culture-changing stories come from?
2. What if the story you need to build isn't authentic to your values?
3. Do you have to star in every culture-changing story?
4. How do you know if the story you are building really breaks with the past?
5. How do you know if your stories provide the right amount of a path to the future?
6. How do you know if your story will appeal to your employees' heads?
7. How do you build a story that appeals to your employees' hearts?
8. Where do the theatrical elements of culture-changing stories come from?
9. How do you get others to build their own stories?

you need to implement. Thus, these stories are not built out of whole cloth, but are grounded in experiences that you and your people share.

For this reason, there is often a bit of serendipity at the beginning of a story-building process—an accident, a failure, a mistake, a funny story that can be used to build a much larger narrative that, in the end, becomes a culture-changing story.

For Manoel Amorim (Story 1.1) it was a product service failure. For Michael Schutzler (Story 4.2) it was posting a list of his preferred values on the wall. For Alberto Carvalho (Story 4.4) it was being too far away from customers in developing economies. For Melanie Healey (Story 5.2) it was not putting enough focus on delighting the customer. For Jeff Rodek (Story 7.1) it was missing fourth-quarter financials. All these business leaders, and many others in the book, found the basic materials needed to build a story when their expectations about what their organization needed to do were inconsistent with what it was actually doing.

So, the answer to the question about where culture-changing stories come from is: They come from your real-life experiences in your organization. Every time you become aware of a time when your organization does not deliver on its strategy, there is a possible culture-changing story there.

As your culture-change process matures, you will be able to use successes created by your culture change to build additional culture-change stories. These stories will reinforce the progress you have made in changing your culture and highlight the positive performance implications of this progress. In the beginning of culture change, you normally will get material for story building from business failures, not successes. But this is only the beginning of story building. Given this start, your task is to build a story that has the attributes described in this book. While you may have little control over the serendipitous beginnings of your story, you have a great deal of control over the shape that this story finally takes.

Indeed, we know business leaders who, once they see the potential of building a culture-changing story, write down an outline of the story they might want to build. They make sure that the story they are going to build has the essential elements of any good story—setting, characters, plot, conflict, and resolution. They then revise that outline to increase the extent to which it reflects the six attributes of culture-changing stories listed in this book. As long as this story-planning process does not make your story inauthentic, it can be helpful in building effective culture-change stories.

Organizational serendipity makes the beginning of your story real. Building a story so that it reflects the story attributes listed in this book makes your story real powerful.

One approach we have seen business leaders use to identify potential culture-changing stories is to spend time once a week writing down all the mistakes, surprises, and misjudgments they experienced at work during the previous seven days. This is essentially "business journaling." Some of these experiences will be the result of simple miscommunication or incompetence. Others will reflect differences in taste and judgment. However, some may reflect cultural values that are getting in the way of you getting the work done. If such a pattern begins to emerge, you may be able to use one of these cultural mishaps as the basis of building a culture-changing story.

What If the Story You Need to Build Isn't Authentic to Your Values?

Culture change is subject to two constraints. On the one hand, the culture you seek to create must be aligned with the strategies you need to implement. If this is not the case, then your new culture will not enable you to implement your new strategies, and thus cannot help you realize competitive advantage.

On the other hand, the culture you seek to create must also be aligned with your own personal values. If this is not the case, then people in your organization will not believe that you are fully committed to culture change, and such change will not be forthcoming.

Unfortunately, there is no guarantee that the culture you need to implement your new strategies will also be consistent with your personal values. Indeed, as was suggested in Chapter 3, you may have been attracted to work at an organization because of its old culture, only to discover that new strategies require a different culture with which you are not altogether comfortable.

In this situation, you really only have two choices: Change your personal values or remove yourself from the culture-change process.

Neither of these are particularly attractive alternatives. The first requires deep personal change, introspection, the reformation of long-held beliefs, and so forth. Of course, if you share these efforts with your employees, they can actually be a great source of culture-changing stories. However, this is small compensation for the emotional challenges typically associated with this kind of personal change.[2]

Removing yourself from the culture-change process can take a variety of forms—you can shift to a part of your organization that requires less culture change, you can take on a role in the current part of your organization that keeps you apart from culture change, you can even leave the company for an opportunity that is more consistent with your values.

If you stay with your organization, removing yourself from the culture-change process may be the equivalent of removing yourself from the most innovative and creative parts of your company. In this case, you get to watch from the sidelines as your organization chooses and implements new strategies with a new culture. If you leave your organization, you run the risk of joining another firm only to discover that they too are entering into a period of culture change.

All that said, the "authenticity" constraint in the culture-change process may mean that you are not the right person to lead a culture change. It requires enormous self-discipline, along with personal courage, to come to this conclusion and to do what needs to be done to enable your organization to implement its new strategies through changing its culture.

Do You Have to Star in Every Culture-Changing Story?

Our research suggests that it is critical for business leaders to star in at least some of the culture-changing stories they build. However, the idea that these leaders need to enroll people throughout an organization in the culture-change process by encouraging them to build their own stories suggests that these leaders do not need to star in all these stories. Indeed, it may be the case that a business leader can star in too many stories—that it becomes more about the business leader starring than it is about culture change.

Indeed, once you have starred in a story or two, you can play a very important role in helping other people in your organization build their own culture-changing stories, stories in which they star. This behind-the-scenes work can be very important for the success of culture change.

Every few years, the Academy of Motion Picture Arts and Sciences Board of Governors gives the Irving G. Thalberg Memorial Award to "creative producers whose bodies of work reflect a consistently high quality of motion picture production." But who was Irving Thalberg?[3]

In a business where "starring in your own story" is taken to new heights, Irving Thalberg never starred in a movie, sang any songs, or danced any dances. Instead, as a producer at MGM in the 1920s and 1930s, Thalberg assembled the talent needed to tell some of the best-loved stories of all time—including *The Hunchback of Notre Dame* (1923), *Ben-Hur* (1925), *The Champ* (1931), *Tarzan the Ape Man* (1932), *Mutiny on the Bounty* (1935), *Romeo and Juliet* (1936), *Camille* (1936), and *The Good Earth* (1937). Nominated for 12 Best Picture Academy Awards—of which he won 2—Thalberg was also known for helping build the careers of many well-known actors, including Lon Chaney, Greta Garbo, Lionel Barrymore, Joan Crawford, Clark Gable, Jean Harlow, and Spencer Tracy. Winners of the Thalberg Award include David O. Selznick, Walt Disney, Cecil B. De-Mille, Alfred Hitchcock, Ingmar Bergman, Steven Spielberg, George Lucas, Clint Eastwood, and Kathleen Kennedy (president of Lucasfilm).

All of this for a person who never starred in his own story. But while Thalberg did not star in his own stories, he knew how to help others star in their stories!

Thus, after you have starred in a couple of culture-changing stories you built, you can begin to play Irving Thalberg's role and help people star in their own culture-changing stories. In fact, it might be a good idea to generate a list of managers at different levels in your organization who would be really good at building and starring in a culture-change story. When the time comes, tap these people on the shoulder and invite them to be part of the culture-change process by building their own story. This is an example of the story-seeding process described in Chapter 8.

How Do You Know If the Story You Are Building Really Breaks with the Past?

To make sure that the stories you are building break with the past, you need to understand your old culture and how your story helps build a culture that is different from this old culture.

Some organizations we know have spent considerable time and money trying to understand their old cultures. They have interviewed hundreds of employees, sent out thousands of surveys, and subjected all this data to rigorous qualitative and quantitative analysis, all to identify the three or four central values of the firm's culture.[4]

We suppose that this effort can be helpful in enabling you to understand your old culture. However, our experience suggests that, for the purpose of facilitating culture change, it is often enough to run a simple experiment that will help you identify at least some of the values of your old culture, and how a story you might build does or does not break with that old culture.

Here is the experiment: Share the story you are planning on building with an experienced member of your organization who is steeped in your organization's traditional culture and watch his or her response. Are they confused? Do they get angry? Are they dismissive? Do they see nothing but trouble if you implement your story? Do they suggest many reasons why the story will not have the desired effects? Do they seem nervous about your story idea?

If you observe any or all of these responses, then you are probably on the right track for building a story that breaks with the past. The initial re-action of people who are well steeped in your organization's traditional culture to a culture-changing story is almost always negative. Thus, these responses can indicate that the story you are thinking about building does break with your organization's cultural past.

Of course, you don't want to ignore these negative responses. You can learn from them and anticipate sources of resistance to culture change throughout your organization. However, negative responses to potential culture-changing stories are usually not an indication that culture change should not happen. Indeed, such responses often are an indication that culture change should happen.

If, on the other hand, you see none of these responses, then you probably have not yet hit upon a story with culture-changing potential. Either that or your colleague is a very good poker player![5]

How Do You Know If Your Stories Provide the Right Amount of a Path to the Future?

By breaking with the past, your stories almost automatically spell out some vision of your organization's cultural future. Maybe that vision is no more than "Our cultural future is not going to be the same as our cultural past." Or maybe that vision is more specific: "Our cultural future will focus on satisfying our customers" or "developing innovative products."

However specific your cultural vision is, it is important that you don't spell out this cultural future in too much detail. The task is to give the people in your organization a cultural direction to follow—we must become more attuned to our customers' needs, we must become more accepting of the risks associated with innovative failures, we must become more humble and transparent—and then encourage them to "fill in the cultural details" that this direction implies for their own part of your organization.

For example, Telesp needed to develop a customer service–oriented culture that was also less hierarchical and less siloed in nature. The service failure experience that led the CEO to have a call center employee explain to the executive team what had to happen to fix these problems (Story 1.1) set the direction of this cultural change. But through the story cascade that was created in this firm (Story 8.7), thousands of employees within Telesp operationalized what "customer service, less hierarchical, and less siloed" actually meant in their part of the organization.

The business leader in this case could anticipate the need for a new culture. This leader could even anticipate the kinds of values and norms that would likely be important in this culture. However, this person could never have anticipated how this new culture would develop and evolve throughout the organization. It was up to employees throughout the firm to cocreate this culture with the business leader in their own areas of responsibility within the organization.

Spelling out your organization's future cultural details too early in the culture-change process can short-circuit the change process and can make it more difficult to get a new culture diffused throughout your organization.

To see if you have hit the right spot in spelling out your organization's cultural future without overspecifying what that future might be, consider the following exercise. After you have built your first couple of stories, invite several influential people from different parts of your organization to join you to think about the future of the culture in your company. After introductions and instructions, have each of these people independently describe the kind of culture they think will emerge within their part of your organization over the next period of time—say, 18 months—based on the stories you have already built and what they know about your organization's current culture.

Each person in this group must do this exercise on their own. They can write a brief description of what the culture might be. We have seen particularly clever business leaders ask people to draw a picture of what they think that culture might be.

After a few minutes, have each person share their vision of the future of culture at your organization. Some will suggest that the organization's culture will not change—a rational expectation, given the low success rate of culture-change initiatives in most organizations. Others will have their own visions of this future, which may or may not be related to the stories you have built.

Evaluate these visions. Are they all seemingly unrelated? Are they all exactly the same? Neither of these extremes is good, since the former suggests that your story building has not yet had any real impact, while the latter suggests that it has had too much of an impact. The sweet spot in this exercise is to see a mix—with some overlap among these cultural visions, but enough heterogeneity to suggest that there is still room to enroll these people to cocreate this culture.

Based on these results, you may want to try to build a consensus about the future culture in your organization—after all, you have already built a couple of stories, so there should be some emerging sense of what this future may look like. You may also want to use this as an opportunity to invite these people to build their own culture-changing stories.

In any case, this experience will give you some sense if you have provided a path to the future, without overspecifying what that path should look like.

How Do You Know If Your Story Will Appeal to Your Employees' Heads?

Culture change that is not a solution to a real business problem does not appeal to your employees' heads. That is, it does not appeal to the rational and profit-maximizing aspects of their intellect. Culture change that does not appeal to your employees' heads will often be dismissed as a business leader's ego trip, no more than an opportunity for that leader to build an organization in his or her likeness.

Of course, to avoid this problem, you need to link the stories you build to change your culture to the strategies you need to implement. Indeed, if you cannot show a direct link between the need for strategic change and the need for cultural change, then you are probably not yet ready to begin the culture-change process. If you can build this link, then you will provide a rational, self-interested reason for people in your organization to join with you in culture change, since doing so will improve the performance of your organization and create new opportunities for your employees.

To see if the stories you are thinking about building are likely to appeal to your employees' heads, go back to that colleague we mentioned earlier—the one who was steeped in your organization's traditional culture. Explain to this colleague why the traditional strategies of your organization are not likely to work going forward. Then describe the new strategies you think will be required and the kind of culture you will need to implement those strategies.

If this colleague's initial reactions to the story you are building—fear, bewilderment, anger, befuddlement—moderate to become cautious optimism, then maybe you have a story that will appeal to your employees' heads.[6]

How Do You Build a Story That Appeals to Your Employees' Hearts?

Appealing to the heart—a person's emotions—is just as important as appealing to the head—a person's rationality—in creating culture change. However, these two ways of thinking are housed in different parts of the brain, and building a story that appeals to both can be challenging.[7] Just as the emotional side of your brain is getting ready to go all in on a profound cultural change, the rational part of your brain can interfere—"Hold on now, emotions. What does this culture change mean for me?"

The challenge here is to build a story that is completely consistent with rational profit-maximizing thought, but that also appeals to the emotions of your people. There is, of course, a great deal of research in psychology and marketing, to name just two areas where this work is done, about how one can influence people to substitute emotional thinking for rational thinking—"I just absolutely need to buy that car!" But culture change is about both heads *and* hearts, not about swapping hearts *for* heads, or even choosing between heads *or* hearts.

To appeal to heads *and* hearts, it is important to build a rational argument for the need for culture change and then to augment—but not contradict—that argument with an appeal to "higher" not self-interested motives:

- "Yes, our new culture will help us sell more products. But the resulting revenue growth will also help our people realize their full leadership potential."
- "Yes, our new culture will enable more innovation. But this innovation will also benefit the lives of our customers and society as a whole."
- "Yes, our new culture will help us reduce costs. But this will enable us to sell our products at even lower prices, which will help our customers."

These sets of statements can be logically consistent with each other. They can even have the added benefit of being true.

So, given that you have been able to develop a rational argument for culture change, how can you augment that argument with an emotional appeal? The list of things that can create emotional appeal is long and diverse. A quick perusal of YouTube suggests that the best thing you could do is to somehow link your culture change to the welfare of babies—human, dog, cat, panda, it doesn't seem to matter much. But this cynical view is inconsistent with the authenticity requirements of culture change discussed earlier in this chapter and in Chapter 3.

In particular, whatever emotional appeals you incorporate into your culture-change efforts must not only be linked with your rational arguments for culture change, they must also be things you care deeply about. In this sense, appealing to the hearts of your employees is every bit as autobiographical as any other element of the culture-change process.

As you contemplate how to reach out to the hearts of your employees, to engage them in culture change, reflect on what moves you. What are the "better angels" of your nature, as Lincoln put it? To the extent that you can link these reasons for culture change with your rational logic, the more likely you will be able to reach out to both the heads and hearts of your employees.

Where Do the Theatrical Elements of Culture-Changing Stories Come From?

Most of the theatrical culture-changing stories presented in this book had one thing in common: they used already scheduled meetings as an opportunity to introduce theater into the culture-change management process. Manoel Amorim used his scheduled executive committee meeting to introduce the call center employee (Story 1.1). Dan Burton used scheduled all-hands meetings to demonstrate transparency about his 360-degree reviews (Story 3.5). Dennis Robinson used a scheduled team meeting to send a message to senior managers that they shouldn't be late (Story 5.1). Mike Staffieri described how DaVita used annual meetings and training graduation meetings to change that organization's culture (Stories 5.6 and 7.6). And Jeff Rodek used an annual celebration meeting to introduce humility into his organization's culture (Story 7.1).

You already have many scheduled meetings in your organization. If we are honest with ourselves, most of these are pretty inconsequential. Many could be replaced by emails. But if you turn these meetings into theatrical events that help drive home the need for culture change, then the meetings suddenly become memorable. And it is impossible to replace those kinds of meetings with emails.

Adding theater to regularly scheduled meetings will take discipline and creativity on your part. There will be, of course, a learning curve in running these kinds of meetings. Some of the business leaders we spoke to started by introducing theater into only a single meeting a year—just enough to see if they could actually do it. Usually, this one experience led to additional experiences.

We also found that if a business leader didn't feel comfortable with their ability to add theater to a meeting, they found help from creative people in their own organization.

Of course, adding theatricality to your meetings can have diminishing returns. If, at some point, a meeting becomes about the theater, rather than about gaining and sustaining competitive advantages, then it probably makes sense to dial back the theater a bit. However, until then, it might be helpful for you to identify one or two meetings each year where you can add some theatricality in ways that help change the culture of your organization.

How Do You Get Others to Build Their Own Stories?

Story cascades are essential for culture change. But how do you get others in your organization to build their own stories? Our research suggests three things you can do.

First, build multiple culture-changing stories in which you star. One story can be a one-off exception. Two stories—your commitment to culture change is a bit stronger. Three or more stories—now you are setting an example. With that example, people throughout your organization will feel more comfortable about building their own stories.

Second, ask people in your organization to build stories. Explain to them the importance of story building in culture change. Talk to them about the attributes of a successful culture-changing story. Of course, you cannot build a story for them—that story would be inauthentic, and thus not successful. But with your coaching, they can learn how to build great culture-changing stories.

Finally, celebrate the stories that are built throughout your organization. Share them broadly. Emphasize their importance in reinforcing culture change. Give bonuses, promotions, and prizes to individuals and teams that build culture-changing stories.

Our research suggests that these actions will often build a story cascade in your company.

Conclusion

This then is how you change your organization's culture. You start by identifying the ways that your current culture is misaligned with the strategies your organization must pursue to be successful. Then you build stories that exemplify the kinds of values and norms a new culture—that actually enables strategy implementation—must have. After you build these stories (with the attributes listed in the book), you then encourage the development of a story cascade throughout your organization. Finally, as this new culture is being cocreated with your employees, you align the other elements of your organization with this new culture. Done and dusted, right?

Of course, actual culture change is never this linear and logical. We are, after all, talking about changing the social underpinnings of your organization—the often-unspoken values and norms that guide employee behavior. As described in Chapter 2, culture change is inherently difficult and challenging. It will rarely be linear. It will rarely be logical.

However, our research suggests that culture change is possible. And the secret to culture change is building stories that exemplify the culture you want to create. If these stories are authentic, star you as the business leader, demonstrate a clear break with the past and a path to the future, appeal to your employees' heads and hearts, are theatrical in nature, and lead to the development of a story cascade, then they can be used to create culture change.

And here is something that we heard in virtually every one of our interviews. Despite its ups and downs and its meandering ways, almost every one of the business leaders we interviewed told us that changing the culture of their organization was among the most rewarding and satisfying experiences in their entire career.

Have fun building your own stories.

Discussion Guide

The Secret to Culture Change

Chapter One: *Building Stories to Change Your Organization's Culture*

1. The chapter begins by suggesting that organizations where strategy and culture align outperform organizations where strategy and culture do not align. Can you think of examples where an organization's strategy and culture are well aligned and that organization still performs poorly, or where an organization's strategy and culture are not well aligned, and it still performs well? How can you reconcile these examples with the assertion in Chapter 1?

2. The chapter asserts that questions of cultural and strategic alignment are important in all types of organizations, including not-for-profit organizations and government agencies. Do you agree with this assertion? If yes, why? If no, why not?

3. The chapter identifies two options—besides changing your culture—if an organization's strategies and culture are misaligned: Change the strategies or try to ignore this misalignment. Are there other alternatives? If yes, what are they? If no, why not?

4. Do you agree with John Kotter's view about culture change? Why or why not?

5. The central assertion of the book is that to change an organization's culture, you must change the stories that employees in the organization share about that organization's values and norms. Do you agree or disagree with this assertion?

6. What is the difference between talking about culture change, "walking" the culture change you want to create, and "walking that talks" about culture change? Are these differences important?

7. What are the differences between story building and storytelling?

8. If you had been the phone center employee that Manoel Amorim had invited to address the corporate executive committee (in Story 1.1),

how would you have responded? In particular, under what conditions would you have gone to the meeting?

9. Do you think that there is an ideal organizational culture that all organizations should aspire to? If yes, what are the characteristics of that culture? If no, why not?

10. Do you think story building is "ethically neutral"? If yes, why? If no, why not?

11. In Andy Theurer's story (Story 1.2, "Was It Cheese or a Doughnut?"), do you think that it matters that the story evolved from the original facts—about one employee stealing another employee's cheese—to the new facts about an employee taking a doughnut out of a box of doughnuts in the break room? Why or why not?

12. Are organizational myths important in companies where you have worked? What are some examples of these myths, and why were they important or not?

Chapter Two: *Why Culture Change Is Different*

1. Can you think of a time when a top-down change process was used in an organization where you worked? How well did that go? How about a bottom-up change process? How well did that go?

2. Can you think of a time when a logical and rational approach to change management was used in an organization where you worked? How well did that go? How about a personal and emotional change process? How well did that go?

3. If organizations are systems, then changing any one element of an organization is going to affect other elements of that organization. In your view, is that likely to make changing an organization more difficult or less difficult?

4. This book espouses an eclectic approach to managing culture change. But to the extent that different change models make contradictory recommendations about how to manage change, how can you reconcile these differences? For example, a rational and logical approach to change generally assumes that the big impediment to change is that people throughout an organization simply do not understand why a change is necessary—that if they understood, then change

would be forthcoming quickly. The personal and emotional approach recognizes that there might be a lack of understanding, but even if this problem were resolved, different people might still react differently to a proposed change. Thus, in this model, explaining why a change is needed may not lead to change.

5. Why is it the case that if *everyone* is in charge of something, then *no one* is in charge of that thing?

6. If an organization's culture is just a "social construct" that has no reality independent of what people in an organization think and feel, is it really possible to manage and change culture? Why or why not?

7. By definition, all change threatens an organization's status quo. Is culture change more or less threatening to this status quo than other kinds of organizational changes you can think of?

8. Why are most people resistant to change? Do you know people who are not resistant to change?

9. When will a series of quick culture-change wins turn into an overall broader scale culture change? When will this not happen?

10. How can you tell the difference between a business leader who is engaging in "cheap talk" and a business leader who is actually committed to culture change?

11. Will culture-changing stories always diffuse across levels and boundaries in an organization? What barriers, if any, might exist to this process? Also, suppose stories do diffuse throughout an organization, is it likely that everyone who hears these stories will interpret them the same way? Why or why not?

Chapter Three: *Building Authentic Stories*

1. Why is building authentic stories so risky, personally and professionally?

2. Have you ever had the kind of insightful experience as the business leader in Story 3.1? What happened, and what impact did that have on your approach to leadership?

3. Why do you think Michael Schutzler (Story 3.2) had the courage to admit his mistakes and start the meeting over? Would you have this same courage?

4. Do you think business leaders are more likely or less likely to be influenced by how other people think about them than people who are not business leaders? Why?

5. How would you have responded to Stefano Rettore's (Story 3.3) decision to start his first business meeting by talking about his life growing up and how it affected his leadership approach? Would you have been comfortable or uncomfortable in this meeting?

6. When was the last time you were treated unfairly by a business leader? How did you respond? Could you have confronted your leader, as in Story 3.4? If not, why not? If you did confront your leader, how did that go?

7. Would you be willing to share your 360-degree reviews with all your colleagues (see Story 3.5). Why or why not?

8. Have you ever known a business leader who concluded that they were not the right person for the job? What decision did they make about continuing in this position or not?

9. Put yourself in Steve Young's position (Story 3.6)—what would you have done when the company founder threw a chair at you?

Chapter Four: *Star in Your Own Story*

1. In Chapter 2, it was suggested that business leaders must be open to a new organizational culture being cocreated with their employees—if not, then culture-change efforts could easily look like a business leader ego trip. In this chapter, it is suggested that business leaders must star in their own stories—which sounds like a business leader ego trip. Can you resolve this tension?

2. Do historical examples, funny stories, and inspirational examples have no role to play in the story-building process? If yes, why? If no, what role can they play?

3. What do you think Annette Friskopp (Story 4.1) was learning about the business, and about herself, on her visits to New Orleans and Houston?

4. What change management process did Michael Schutzler try to employ to create a culture at Freeshop (Story 4.2). Why did this effort fail?

5. If you were reporting to the plant manager in Story 4.3, how would you have responded when he took responsibility for the failed prod-

uct introduction? Would you have admired him for his courage, or thought he was foolish for accepting responsibility for what was almost certainly someone else's mistake?

6. Gillette is a well-known and successful company (Story 4.4). Why did it never occur to anyone in the company to go and visit developing economies to see why their products were not selling?

7. Role-play the situation Jamie O'Banion (Story 4.5) found herself in—selling beauty products on national television with a giant gash in your eyebrow. What would you say to take what looks like a problem and turn it into an opportunity?

Chapter Five: *Stories That Break with the Past, with a Path toward the Future*

1. How would you feel if you were in the meeting where a senior manager is locked out for being late (Story 5.1)?

2. Do you think it was important that Melanie Healey (Story 5.2) had customers physically sort products into those that were and were not "delightful"? Why or why not?

3. The purpose of empowering women through their feminine care products seems noble. Why was this purpose, by itself, not enough to change the product design culture in the feminine care division at P&G (Story 5.2)?

4. Generate a list of all the things that Ivan Filho (Story 5.3) did to change the culture at his Tenneco business unit. Which of these actions do you think were the most important in changing the culture of that organization? Why?

5. How would you have responded when those two employees came to you and demanded a raise (Story 5.4)? Why was Michael Speigl willing and able to stand up to them?

6. Why is cost reduction so much easier than culture change (Story 5.5)?

7. Why is symbolic imagery—like crossing a bridge (Story 5.6)—so important in culture change?

Chapter Six: *Build Stories for the Head and Heart*

1. Which do you think is the bigger mistake—focusing only on the head in making culture change or focusing only on the heart in making culture change? Why?
2. Fernando Aguirre (Story 6.1) alternated between head and heart approaches to culture change. Do you see this as an effective approach to culture change, or just confusing to his employees?
3. What conditions had to exist in order for Marise Barroso's efforts to change the culture of her company (Story 6.2) to actually work?
4. Scott Robinson (Story 6.3) was only 23 years old when he was asked to change the culture of the negotiation with the union. In what ways was his age a weakness in changing this culture? In what ways was it a strength?
5. Firms like DaVita (Story 6.4) are sometimes criticized for making employee well-being more important than profit generation. Do you agree or disagree with this criticism? Why?

Chapter Seven: *Story Building as Theater*

1. Have you ever had a business leader engage in the kinds of theatrics described in this chapter? If yes, did your respect for this leader increase, decrease, or remain unchanged? Why?
2. Which of the stories in this chapter do you think were likely to be the most successful in changing an organization's culture? Why?
3. How would you feel about dressing up as Steven Tyler? (See Story 7.4.) Why?
4. To engage in these kinds of theatrics, do you think a business leader needs to be an extrovert? If yes, does this mean that extroversion is an unstated requirement for business leaders to change their cultures? If no, how can introverts learn how to become more theatrical?

Chapter Eight: *Creating a Story Cascade*

1. In your view, which is better for culture change—a story that "shares itself" or a story that is proactively shared by a business leader in a meeting or on the web? Why?

2. How do you know when your efforts to share a culture-changing story begin to undermine the authenticity of that story?

3. Why is it that sometimes all-hands meetings can create catchphrases—like "stop lifting the pig" (Story 8.1)—that facilitate culture change? What could you do to increase the likelihood that this will occur?

4. How did Pete Pizarro (Story 8.2) make sure that his small group meetings became a model for the kind of culture he wanted to create rather than just an opportunity for him to bring attention to his "from rags to riches" story?

5. Do you think it is appropriate for a CEO to give feedback directly to people who are building and revising a product (Story 8.3)? What about the chain of command?

6. Do you think 50 hours of phone calls (Story 8.4) was really a good investment of time for this senior manager?

7. Can you build too many stories too fast? How can you tell if this is happening?

8. How do you make sure if you ask others in your organization to build stories that the stories they build are authentic to them and not just parroting stories you have already built?

9. The VP of sales at Traeger is the one who initially heard about Rob's "no reservations" service (Story 8.5), and he enthusiastically shared this story with the CEO. What if someone in accounting or finance had heard this story? Would their response have been the same or different? After all, it is unlikely that Traeger made money from Rob's "no reservations" decision.

10. Both Jeremy Andrus (Story 8.6) and Manoel Amorim (Story 8.7) compensated people for building culture-changing stories. How does this affect the authenticity of these stories and thus their ability to actually facilitate culture change?

Chapter Nine: *Making Culture Change Stick*

1. Given that your old policies and practices are usually aligned with your old culture, why doesn't it make sense to start culture change by altering these policies and practices to be consistent with the culture you want to build, instead of starting culture change with story building?

2. Your HR managers usually have years of experience in hiring people based on their job-specific skills. Hiring based on a potential employee's values is relatively new. Why should your HR people abandon well-established competence-based hiring practices for not-so-well-established values-based hiring practices?

3. Do you think training can change a person's values? What does your answer to this question say about the relationship between your hiring practices and training?

4. Employee scorecards (Story 9.1) are only as good as the measures they include. What are some measures of customer satisfaction that could have been used on employee scorecards at Telesp?

5. Manoel Amorim (Story 9.1) was not the only business leader we interviewed who shared his 360-degree evaluations with his entire organization (see Dan Burton in Story 3.5). Would you be willing to share your 360-degree evaluations? Why or why not?

6. Compensation systems create "winners" and "losers" in your organization (see Story 9.2). Do you think this hurts or helps culture change?

7. How would you feel if you had to terminate people because they could not or would not support a culture change—even if they had been successful in your organization's old culture? How would you feel if you were one of these terminated people? Would these feelings hurt or help culture-change efforts?

Chapter Ten: *How to Build Your Own Culture-Changing Stories*

1. Why isn't it possible for this book to generate a list of stories you need to build in order to change your culture?

2. Why are business failures more likely to be sources of culture-changing stories at the beginning of this process, and business success more likely to be sources of such stories toward the end of this process?

3. Are there limits to the extent to which you can plan your culture-changing stories? If yes, why and what are these limits? If no, why not?

4. Keep a journal of all the business experiences you have in a week. Then look back on this list and identify those that may have potential to turn into a culture-changing story.

5. How can you tell the difference between a business leader who is orchestrating the building of culture-changing stories from behind the scenes and a business leader who is simply not engaged in culture-changing efforts?

6. Do you agree or disagree with this statement? "The more time and energy an organization spends describing its current culture, the less likely it will be to change that culture."

7. Many business leaders like to be in detailed control of organizational change efforts. Suppose your business leader wanted to maintain this kind of control in changing your organizational culture. What would you tell this leader to convince them that this would be a self-defeating exercise?

8. Take a few minutes and draw a picture of what the culture of your organization will look like in 18 months. Is it the same as your current culture, or is it different in some ways?

9. What are the limitations of rational logic in implementing culture change?

10. What are the limitations of emotional appeals in implementing culture change?

Notes

Chapter One

1. For several examples of the emergence of disruptive technologies, see Clayton Christensen, *The Innovator's Dilemma* (Boston: Harvard Business Review Press, 1997).
2. For a discussion of the evolution of the economic development sector of the world economy, see William Easterly, *The White Man's Burden* (New York: Penguin, 2006); and C. K. Prahalad, *The Fortune at the Bottom of the Pyramid* (Philadelphia: Wharton, 2005).
3. See, for example, Tom Peters and Robert Waterman Jr., *In Search of Excellence: Lessons from America's Best-Run Companies* (New York: Harper & Row, 1982); Jim Collins and Jerry Porras, *Built to Last: Successful Habits of Visionary Companies* (New York: HarperCollins, 1994); and Jim Collins, *Good to Great: Why Some Companies Make the Leap . . . and Others Don't* (New York: HarperCollins, 2001).
4. This logic is explored in Jay Barney, "Organizational Culture: Can It Be a Source of Sustained Competitive Advantage?" *Academy of Management Review* 11 (1986): 656–665. On the cultural underpinnings of innovation strategies, see Gaylen Chandler, Chalon Keller, and Douglas Lyon, "Unraveling the Determinants and Consequences of Innovation-Supportive Organizational Culture," *Entrepreneurship: Theory and Practice* 25, no. 1 (2000): 59–76. On product quality strategies, see Ashwin Srinivasan and Bryan Kurey, "Creating a Culture of Quality," *Harvard Business Review*, April 2014, 23–25. On customer service strategies, see Benjamin Schneider, Susan White, and Michelle Paul, "Linking Service Climate and Customer Perceptions of Service Quality: Test of a Causal Model," *Journal of Applied Psychology* 83, no. 2 (1998): 150–163. These have been widely documented.
5. Ironically, this is often not the case. See William Easterly, *The White Man's Burden* (New York: Penguin, 2006).
6. For a discussion of the relationship between a firm's strategy and competitive advantage, see Jay Barney and Bill Hesterly, *Strategic Management and Competitive Advantage*, 6th ed. (New York: Pearson, 2019).
7. John Kotter, *Leading Change* (Boston: Harvard Business Review Press, 2012), 164–165.
8. See, for example, Siobhan McHale, *The Insider's Guide to Culture Change: Creating a Workplace That Delivers, Grows, and Adapts* (New York: HarperCollins Leadership, 2020); Michael Fullan, *Leading in a Culture Change*, 2nd ed. (San Francisco: Jossey-Bass, 2020); Daniel Denison et al., *Leading Culture Change in Global Organizations* (San Francisco: Jossey-Bass, 2012); Christopher Dawson,

Leading Culture Change: What Every CEO Needs to Know (Stanford, CA: Stanford University Press, 2010).

9. These change management models are discussed in Chapter 2.

10. See Alan Wilkins, *Developing Corporate Character: How to Successfully Change an Organization Without Destroying It* (San Francisco: Jossey-Bass, 1991); Alan Wilkins, "The Creation of Company Cultures: The Role of Stories and Human Resource Systems," *Human Resource Management* 23, no. 1 (1984): 41–60; and Terrence Deal and Allan Kennedy, *Corporate Cultures: The Rites and Rituals of Corporate Life* (Reading, MA: Addison-Wesley, 1982).

11. The importance of storytelling is discussed in a wide variety of sources, including, for example, Paul Smith, *Lead with a Story* (New York: American Management Association, 2012); Paul Smith, *The 10 Stories Great Leaders Tell* (Naperville, IL: Simple Truths, 2019); Ryan Mathews and Watts Wacker, *What's Your Story? Storytelling to Move Markets, Audiences, and Brands* (Upper Saddle River, NJ: FT Press, 2008); Craig Wortmann, *What's Your Story? Using Stories to Ignite Performance and Be More Successful* (New York: Kaplan, 2006); Evelyn Clark, *Around the Corporate Campfire: How Great Leaders Use Stories to Inspire Success* (Sevierville, TN: Insight, 2004); Chip Heath and Dan Heath, *Made to Stick* (London: Penguin, 2007); Mike Adams, *Seven Stories Every Salesperson Must Tell* (Matthews, NC: Kona, 2018); Lori Silverman, *Wake Me Up When the Data Is Over: How Organizations Use Stories to Inspire Success* (San Francisco: Jossey-Bass, 2006); and Bronwyn Fryer, "Storytelling That Moves People," *Harvard Business Review*, June 2003, 5–8.

12. Christopher Booker has argued that there are seven basic stories: Overcome the Monster, Rags to Riches, the Quest, Voyage and Return, Comedy, Tragedy, and Rebirth. See Christopher Booker, *Seven Basic Plots* (New York: Continuum, 2006).

13. These will be discussed in Chapter 9.

14. In short, we did not "select on our dependent variable," a methodological weakness that has limited the implications of many popular business books, including Thomas Peters and Robert Waterman Jr., *In Search of Excellence: Lessons from America's Best-Run Companies* (New York: Harper & Row, 1982). The full details of how we built and analyzed our database are presented in the methodological section of this chapter.

15. Of course, overusing stories like this for marketing purposes can undermine their authenticity, both within an organization and among its external stakeholders. These issues will be discussed in more detail in Chapter 8.

16. This approach to understanding strategy and competitive advantage was first developed in Jay Barney, "Firm Resources and Sustained Competitive Advantage," *Journal of Management* 7 (1991): 49–64.

17. Of course, because not all strategies an organization might pursue are ethically neutral, not all culture-changing stories are ethically neutral. To take an extreme example: The Nazi Party in Germany, before the Second World War, used very powerful story-building tools—including mass rallies, collective mob action, and powerful symbols—to build stories that helped transform the culture of that country. The classic description of these events can be found in William L. Shirer, *The*

Rise and Fall of the Third Reich (New York: Touchstone, 1960). There are also many examples of story building to align a firm's culture with the implementation of deeply unethical strategies. On the use of accounting fraud at Enron, see Bethany McLean and Peter Elkind, *The Smartest Guys in the Room* (New York: Portfolio, 2013). On selling polluting cars at Volkswagen, see Jack Ewing, *Faster, Higher, Farther: The Volkswagen Scandal* (New York: Norton, 2017). On the admissions scandals at many top universities in the United States, see Melissa Korn and Jennifer Levitz, *Unacceptable: Privilege, Deceit, and the Making of the College Admissions Scandal* (New York: Portfolio, 2020). Like any tool, story building can be used for good or ill.

18. Most of the stories in this book directly quote the managers who were interviewed and also reveal the name of the company within which a story was built. However, when managers asked us to not reveal who they or their companies were, these stories were disguised. In these few cases, we start a story with a phrase like "We are familiar with a company that . . ." or "We are familiar with a business leader who . . ." In these cases, the substance of a story in our database is communicated without the specific language that was used to share that story, the name of the person who shared that story, or the name of the company involved.

19. Joseph Campbell, *The Hero with a Thousand Faces* (Novato, CA: New World Library, 1949); Joseph Campbell and Bill Moyers, *The Power of Myth* (New York: Doubleday, 1988); and Maureen Murdock, *The Heroine's Journey* (Boston: Shambhala, 1990).

Chapter Two

1. Examples of more top-down change management models include the eight-stage change process in John Kotter, *Leading Change* (Boston: Harvard Business Review Press, 2012); the "nudge" theory of change in Richard Thaler and Cass Sunstein, *Nudge: Improving Decisions about Health, Wealth, and Happiness* (New York: Penguin, 2008); and work on transformational leadership in Bernard Bass, *Transformational Leadership* (New York: Psychology Press, 1998). Examples of more bottom-up change management models include Robert Kegan and Lisa Lahey's work on individual development and organizational change, and Daniel Coyle's group-based approach to culture change. See Kegan and Lahey, *How the Way We Talk Can Change the Way We Work* (San Francisco: Jossey-Bass, 2001); Kegan and Lahey, *An Everyone Culture: Becoming a Deliberately Developmental Organization* (Boston: Harvard Business Review Press, 2016); and Coyle, *The Culture Code* (New York: Bantam, 2018).

2. Examples of organizational change models that rely more on personal and emotional change include applications of Elisabeth Kubler-Ross's theory of grieving to responses to organizational change, Simon Sinek's work on finding purpose in work, and Judith Glaser's work on creating cooperative thinking in organizations. See Kubler-Ross, *On Death and Dying* (New York: Simon & Schuster, 1969);

Sinek, *Start with Why* (New York: Penguin, 2009); and Glaser, *Creating We* (Avon, MA: Platinum, 2005). Examples of work that focuses more on rationality and logic in creating organizational change include David Garvin and Michael Roberto, "Change through Persuasion," *Harvard Business Review*, February 2005, 26–34; W. Chan Kim and Renee Mauborgne, "Tipping Point Leadership," *Harvard Business Review*, April 2003, 60–69; and Harold Sirkin, Perry Keenan, and Alan Jackson, "The Hard Side of Change Management," *Harvard Business Review*, October 2005, 99–109.

3. Examples of systems approaches to change management include Jeff Hiatt's ADKAR model, the McKinsey 7-S model of organizational change (first applied by Tom Peters and Robert Waterman), and Will Scott's work on culture change. See Hiatt, *ADKAR: A Model for Change in Business, Government, and Community* (Loveland, CO: Prosci Learning Center, 2006); Peters and Waterman, *In Search of Excellence* (New York: Harper, 1982); and Scott, *The Gift of Culture* (Chicago: Culture Czars, 2002).

4. It follows that efforts to change other elements of an organization that share some of these attributes with organizational culture could also be effectively managed using this eclectic approach. For a discussion of the advantages, and disadvantages, of an eclectic approach to organizational change, see Michael Beer, Russell Eisenstat, and Bert Spector, "Why Change Programs Don't Produce Change," *Harvard Business Review*, November-December 1990, 112–121.

5. Some organizations do have "vice presidents of culture." However, while people in these roles often have responsibility for describing and maintaining a firm's culture, they are rarely in a position to take the lead in changing a firm's culture to align with its strategies.

6. The idea that socially created phenomena, like an organization's culture, can still have real effects has been explored in philosophy by, among others, John Searle, *The Construction of Social Reality* (New York: Free Press, 1997).

7. This concept was first introduced by Hiroyuki Itami and Thomas Roehl, *Mobilizing Invisible Assets* (Cambridge, MA: Harvard University Press, 1991).

8. Robert Kegan and Lisa Lahey, *Immunity to Change* (Boston: Harvard Business Review Press, 2009); Rosabeth Moss Kanter, "Ten Reasons People Resist Change," *Harvard Business Review*, September 25, 2012, https://hbr.org/2012/09/ten-reasons -people-resist-chang.html.

9. This story is from David Kearn, *Prophets in the Dark* (New York: HarperCollins, 1993), 82.

10. Nora Eckert, "At Ford, Quality Is Now Problem 1," *Wall Street Journal*, August 6, 2022.

11. Lee Perry and Jay Barney, "Performance Lies Are Hazardous to Organizational Health," *Organizational Dynamics* (Winter 1981): 68–80.

12. While 70 percent of all organizational change efforts fail to meet expectations, the failure rate for cultural change efforts is much higher—81 percent. A more recent study showed that 96 percent of organization-wide transformations fail to meet expectations, and that this is mostly because these organizations were unable to change their culture. The 70 percent failure rate was first cited by Michael

Hammer and James Champy, *Reengineering the Corporation* (New York: Harper Business, 1993), in the context of process reengineering efforts. Failure rates for different kinds of organizational changes were estimated by Martin Smith, "Success Rates for Different Types of Organizational Change," *Performance Improvement* 41, no. 1 (2002): 26–33. The numbers on the rate and cause of company-wide transformation efforts not meeting expectations are from a 2018 study conducted by McKinsey and Company, cited in Siobhan McHale, *The Insider's Guide to Culture Change: Creating a Workplace That Delivers, Grows, and Adapts* (New York: HarperCollins, 2020), 2.

13. The idea of "cheap talk" was first introduced by Vincent Crawford and Joel Sobel, "Strategic Information Transmission," *Econometrica* 50, no. 6 (1982): 1431–1451.

14. "History Timeline: Post-it Notes," Post-it.com, accessed July 21, 2022, https://www.post-it.com/3M/en_US/post-it/contact-us/about-us/.

15. Jeff Thomson, "Company Culture Soars at Southwest Airlines," *Forbes*, December 18, 2018, https://www.forbes.com/sites/jeffthomson/2018/12/18/company-culture-soars-at-southwest-airlines/.

16. Christian Conte, "Nordstrom Customer Service Tales Not Just Legend," Bizjournals.com, accessed July 21, 2022, https://www.bizjournals.com/jacksonville/blog/retail_radar/2012/09/nordstrom-tales-of-legendary-customer.html.

17. Sam Rayburn, former Speaker of the US House of Representatives.

Chapter Three

1. This story is taken from Steve Young, *The Law of Love* (Salt Lake City: Deseret Book, 2022), 111–114.

2. See Stephen E. Ambrose, *Eisenhower: Soldier and President* (New York: Simon & Schuster, 1991).

3. See Michael J. Finnegan, *General Eisenhower's Battle for Control of the Strategic Bombers in Support of Operation Overlord: A Case Study in Unity of Command* (Carlisle, PA: United States War College, 1999); and Geoffrey De Tingo, *Eisenhower's Pursuit of Strategy: The Importance of Understanding the Influence of Leadership Styles on Strategic Decision Makers* (Fort Leavenworth, KS: School of Advanced Military Studies, 2013).

4. On trivialities like this turn to the history of nations!

5. Quoted in Carlos D'Este, *Eisenhower: A Soldier's Life* (New York: Henry Holt, 2002), 499.

6. See Ambrose, *Eisenhower: Soldier and President.*

Chapter Four

1. See R. Guha, *Gandhi: The Years That Changed the World* (New York: Knopf, 2018). Gandhi describes his approach to social and cultural change in his own words in M. Gandhi, *Autobiography: The Story of My Experiments with Truth* (New York: Dover, 1983).

Chapter Five

1. See David M. Gordon, *Apartheid in South Africa: A Brief History with Documents* (London: Bedford, 2017).
2. Mandela's autobiography is Nelson Mandela, *Long Walk to Freedom* (Boston: Back Bay Books, 1995). One excellent biography is Anthony Sampson, *Mandela: The Authorized Biography* (New York: Vintage, 2000).
3. See Chapter 4 in this book.
4. For example, Zimbabwe became an independent nation in 1980, and eliminated many white privileges that had existed previously. Between 1980 and 1990, over two-thirds of the white population of Zimbabwe had left the country. See Alois S. Mlambo, *A History of Zimbabwe* (Cambridge: Cambridge University Press, 2014).
5. Details of the TRC's operations can be found at "South African Truth Commission," Legal Information Institute, accessed November 29, 2022, https://www.law .cornell.edu/wex/south_african_truth_commission.
6. See Jay A. Bora and Erika Vora, "The Effectiveness of South Africa's Truth and Reconciliation Commission: Perceptions of Xhosa, Afrikaner, and English South Africans," *Journal of Black Studies* 34, no. 3 (2004): 301–322.
7. Quote taken from Sampson, *Mandela: The Authorized Biography*, 512.
8. See John Carlin, *Invictus: Nelson Mandela and the Game That Made a Nation* (New York: Penguin, 2008). This story was also told in the 2009 movie *Invictus*, directed by Clint Eastwood, starring Morgan Freeman and Matt Damon.
9. Discussions of controversies associated with Nelson Mandela can be found at Olivia Waxman, "The U.S. Government Had Nelson Mandela on Terrorist Watch Lists Until 2008. Here's Why," *Time*, July 18, 2018, https://time.com/5338569/nelson -mandela-terror-list/; and "For Much of His Life, Mandela Was a Controversial Figure," NPR, December 6, 2013, https://www.npr.org/2013/12/06/249216354/for -much-of-his-life-mandela-was-a-controversial-figure.

Chapter Six

1. Alexander McClure, *Yarns and Stories of Abraham Lincoln* (New York: Walking Lion, 2013).
2. See Doris Kearns Goodwin, *Team of Rivals* (New York: Simon & Schuster, 2005).
3. Goodwin, *Team of Rivals*, 687.
4. Goodwin, *Team of Rivals*, 687.

Chapter Seven

1. See Kurt Lewin, *Resolving Social Conflicts* (New York: Harper & Row, 1949).
2. Stefan Berger and Holger Nehrin, eds., *The History of Social Movements in Global Perspective* (New York: Palgrave Macmillan, 2017).
3. See Eric Metaxas, *Amazing Grace: William Wilberforce and the Heroic Campaign to End Slavery* (New York: HarperOne, 2007).

Chapter Eight

1. Marshall McLuhan, Quentin Fiore, and Jerome Agel, *The Medium Is the Message* (New York: Bantam Books, 1967).
2. See, for example, Ariel Gelrud Shiro and Richard V. Reeves, "The For-Profit College System Is Broken and the Biden Administration Needs to Fix It," Brookings, January 12, 2021, https://brookings.edu/blog/how-we-rise/2021/01/12/the-for -profit-college-system-is-broken-and-the-biden-administration-needs-to-fix-it.
3. This story is taken from Jeremy Andrus, "Traeger's CEO on Cleaning Up a Toxic Culture," *Harvard Business Review*, March/April 2019, 33–37; and from personal interviews with Mr. Andrus.

Chapter Nine

1. For a summary of competence-based approaches to hiring, see Lee Michael Katz, "Competencies Hold the Key to Better Hiring," SHRM, *HR Magazine*, January 29, 2015, https://www.shrm.org/hr-today/news/hr-magazine/pages/0315 -competencies-hiring.aspx.
2. In this particular case, the company in question developed tools for evaluating the personalities of new hires using logic derived from Don Riso, *Personality Types: Using the Enneagram for Self-Discovery* (New York: HarperOne, 1996); and Don Riso and Russ Hudson, *The Wisdom of the Enneagram* (New York: Bantam, 1999).
3. This effect was first discussed by Todd Zenger, "Explaining Organizational Diseconomies of Scale in R&D: Agency Problems and Allocation of Engineering Talent, Ideas, and Effort by Firm Size," *Management Science* 40, no. 6 (1994): 708–729.
4. This pamphlet was later expanded into a book by David Packard, *The HP Way: How Bill Hewlett and I Built Our Company* (New York: Harper Business, 1995).
5. "Our Credo," Johnson & Johnson, accessed January 1, 2023, https://www.jnj .com/credo/.
6. This management philosophy is summarized in Charles Koch, *The Science of Success: How Market-Based Management Built the World's Largest Private Company* (New York: Wiley, 2007).
7. See, for example, Peter Mansoor and Williamson Murray, eds., *The Culture of Military Organizations* (Cambridge: Cambridge University Press, 2019); and Mark Brouker, *Lessons from the Navy* (New York: Rowman & Littlefield, 2020). A broader discussion of these issues can be found in Steve Magness, *Do Hard Things* (New York: HarperOne, 2022).
8. Jim Collins, *Good to Great* (New York: Harper Business, 2001).

Chapter Ten

1. See, for example, Donald M. Murray, "All Writing Is Autobiography," *College Composition and Communication* 42, no. 1 (1991): 66–74.

2. See, for example, Sigmund Freud and Josef Breuer, "Studies in Hysteria," in *The Standard Edition of the Complete Psychological Works of Sigmund Freud*, vol. 2, ed. James Strachey (London: Hogarth, 1895/1955): 1–305; and Shaul Oreg, "Resistance to Change: Developing an Individual Differences Measure," *Journal of Applied Psychology* 88, no. 4 (2003): 680–693.

3. See Mark A. Vieira, *Irving Thalberg: Boy Wonder to Producer Prince* (Los Angeles: University of California Press, 2009).

4. Interestingly, these efforts are usually not a prelude to culture change, but rather are efforts to maintain a firm's current culture by documenting its main elements.

5. Of course, you may want to repeat this experiment several times to get some sense of how generalizable this person's response is. Moreover, this will give you an opportunity to refine your culture-changing story.

6. This should also be repeated several times in your organization before you build your first stories.

7. Simplifying, the rational functions of the brain are located in the prefrontal cortex, while the emotional functions of the brain are located in the limbic system (including the hippocampus and amygdala). See Earl Miller, David Freedman, and Jonathan Wallis, "The Prefrontal Cortex: Categories, Concepts, and Cognition," *Philosophical Transactions of the Royal Society of London, Series B, Biological Sciences* 357, no. 1424 (2002): 1123–1136; and Peter Morgane, Janina Galler, and David Mokler, "A Review of Systems and Networks of the Limbic Forebrain/ Limbic Midbrain," *Progress in Neurobiology* 75, no. 2 (2005): 143–160.

Acknowledgments

This book would not have been possible without . . .

the countless business leaders who, over the years, have shared their culture-changing experiences with us

and

Professor Barney's assistant, Tresa Fish, who somehow kept track of all the transcripts, all the stories, and all the revisions, and always with good humor and patience.

Index

About the Authors

Jay B. Barney

Jay is among the most cited strategic management scholars worldwide. His consulting
work often focuses on implementing strategy
through culture change. He received his Ph.D.
from Yale and currently serves as a Presidential
Professor and the Lassonde Chair of Social Entrepreneurship at the University of Utah.

Manoel Amorim

Manoel was CEO of four large corporations
and board director in six countries. His most
visible culture transformation work was celebrated in a Harvard Business School case and
sparked the idea for this book. He is a Harvard MBA and member of the Marriott
School of Business Advisory Council.

Carlos Júlio

Carlos is a business school professor, corporate
speaker, global executive, author, and board
member. Founder and former CEO of HSM—
the largest management training company in
Latin America—he has published nine books
on management and leadership. His work often
involves helping organizations change their
culture.